Smartsheet for Everyone

Building Skills from Beginner to Advanced Level

Ken Armstrong
Smartsheetdude@gmail.com

The comprehensive guide to harnessing the full potential of one of the most powerful work management platforms available today

SMARTSHEET FOR EVERYONE

First edition. August 8, 2025.

ISBN: 979-8231770014

Written by Ken Armstrong.

Table of Contents

Introduction

Welcome to *Smartsheet for Everyone: Building Skills from Beginner to Advanced Level*, your comprehensive guide to harnessing the full potential of one of the most powerful work management platforms available today.

In an era where collaboration, efficiency, and data-driven decisions define success, Smartsheet stands out as an enterprise-grade tool that transforms how teams plan, execute, and scale their work. At its core, Smartsheet is more than just a spreadsheet it's a dynamic, no-code platform powered by AI that combines real-time collaboration, workflow automation, seamless integrations with your favorite apps, and robust security features. Whether you're tracking projects, automating repetitive tasks, or gaining insights through intelligent formulas and data analysis, Smartsheet empowers businesses like Roche, Uber, and McLaren Racing to manage more with less, drive efficiencies, and accelerate outcomes.

This book is designed for everyone: absolute beginners dipping their toes into digital work management, intermediate users looking to streamline their processes, and advanced professionals aiming to build complex automations and custom solutions. If you're a project manager juggling deadlines, a team lead fostering collaboration, or an executive seeking operational excellence, you'll find practical, step-by-step guidance tailored to your needs.

We'll start with the fundamentals of setting up your first sheet, understanding grids, and basic sharing before progressing to intermediate topics like formulas, reports, and dashboards. Finally, we'll dive into advanced territory: AI-powered tools, custom integrations, automation workflows, and optimization strategies to make Smartsheet a powerhouse for your organization.

By the end of this journey, you'll not only have an advanced understanding of Smartsheet but also unlock new levels of productivity and innovation in your work. Let's get started on your path to Smartsheet expertise!

—Smartsheet Dude

Beginner Level

Chapter 1: What is Smartsheet and Why Use It?

Smartsheet is a powerful, cloud-based platform that blends the simplicity of spreadsheets with advanced project management, collaboration, and automation tools. It's designed for teams to organize work, track projects, manage data, and automate processes without needing coding skills. Unlike basic tools like Excel or Google Sheets, Smartsheet offers real-time collaboration, visual dashboards, forms for data collection, and integrations with other apps, making it ideal for businesses, remote teams, and personal use.

Key Components and How It Works

- **Core Structure**: Everything revolves around "sheets" (like spreadsheets), but you can build "reports" to summarize data from multiple sheets, "dashboards" for visual overviews, and "forms" for easy input.
- **Cloud-Based Advantages**: Access from anywhere via web, mobile apps (iOS/Android), or desktop. Data updates in real-time, with version history to track changes.
- **Use Cases**: Project tracking (e.g., Gantt charts for timelines), task management (e.g., to-do lists with assignments), inventory (e.g., tracking stock levels), event planning (e.g., RSVPs via forms), and CRM (e.g., client pipelines).

Why Use It? Detailed Benefits

- **Ease of Use for Beginners**: Familiar grid interface, but with drag-and-drop features and templates to skip starting from scratch. No steep learning curve if you know spreadsheets, you're 80% there.
- **Collaboration Power**: Multiple users edit simultaneously, with comments, @mentions, and sharing controls to prevent

chaos.

- **Scalability and Security**: Free plan for basics (limited queries/month), paid plans (Pro, Business, Enterprise) for unlimited automations, advanced reporting, and enterprise-grade security like SSO and data encryption.
- **Integrations**: Connects to 100+ tools (e.g., Slack for notifications, Google Drive for attachments, Microsoft Teams for chats).
- **Automation and Efficiency**: Set rules to auto-assign tasks or send alerts, saving hours on repetitive work.

Getting Started Mindset

- **Free Trial**: Sign up for a 30-day Pro trial to test premium features like unlimited viewers and advanced formulas.
- **License Vs Non-License Users**: A licensed user is a paid user who can create new items in Smartsheet, including sheets, reports, and dashboards, and share them with others. A non-licensed user is someone who does not have a paid Smartsheet license. Non-licensed users have the ability to view and/or edit the items they have been shared to, but they do not have the ability to create their own items without a license.
- **Common Beginner Scenario**: A small team managing a marketing campaign use Smartsheet to assign tasks, track deadlines, and visualize progress in a dashboard.
- **Pitfalls to Avoid**: Don't overload your first sheet with too many features; start simple to avoid frustration.

Pro Tip: Explore the Solution Center for 100+ templates tailored to industries like marketing, IT, or HR.

Chapter 2: Signing Up and Your First Login

Getting into Smartsheet is straightforward, but let's break it down with more details on account types, setup options, and initial exploration.

Step-by-Step Signup Process

1. **Visit the Site**: Go to the Smartsheet website and click "Sign Up for Free."
2. **Enter Details**: Provide your email (work recommended for team invites), name, and create a password. Optionally, sign up via Google, Apple, or Microsoft accounts for single sign-on.
3. **Verification**: Check your inbox for a confirmation email and click the link to activate.
4. **Account Type Selection**: As of 2025, choose Free (basic limits), or start a trial of Pro, Business, or Enterprise. Free includes core features but caps automations and attachments.
5. **Initial Setup**: Set your time zone, language (supports 10+ languages), and profile pic. If joining a company account, accept an invite email.

First Login and Home Screen Tour

- **Dashboard Overview**: After login, you'll see the Home tab a personalized hub with recent items, favorites, and a search bar. On the left: Navigation pane for Sheets, Reports, Dashboards, Workspaces (like folders), and Templates.
- **Mobile Setup**: Download the app from App Store or Google Play. Log in with your credentials it mirrors the web but optimized for touch (e.g., swipe to edit rows).
- **Security Basics**: Enable two-factor authentication (2FA) in Account Settings > Security for added protection.

Beginner Exploration Tips

- **Quick Start**: Click "Create New" to make your first sheet, or browse the Learning Center for interactive tutorials.
- **Example**: If you're a freelancer, create a workspace called "Client Projects" to organize sheets by client.
- **Pitfalls**: Forgetting to verify email can lock you out, check spam if needed.

Pro Tip: Use the "Getting Started Checklist" template from the Solution Center to track your learning progress.

Chapter 3: Navigating the Smartsheet Interface

The interface is intuitive, but mastering navigation saves time. Let's detail menus, views, and customization.

Main Elements Breakdown

- **Home Screen**: Central hub with tabs for Home (recents), Browse (all items), Favorites (pinned), and Recents. Use the global search to find anything by keyword.
- **Left Sidebar**: Key sections include Home, Recent, Favorites, Workspaces, Sheets, Reports, Dashboards, Forms, and Settings. Click "+" to create new items.
- **Top Menu Bar**: Icons for notifications (bell for alerts), account (profile for settings), help (question mark for docs), and apps (integrations launcher).
- **Sheet-Specific Tools**: Inside a sheet, see toolbar for views (Grid, Gantt, Card, Calendar), formulas (fx icon), sharing, automation, and export (PDF/Excel).

Views and Customization

- **Switch Views**: Grid for data entry, Gantt for timelines (drag bars to adjust dates), Card for Kanban-style (drag cards between columns), Calendar for events.

- **Personalization**: Pin items to Favorites, enable Dark Mode (Settings > Personal > Theme), or adjust column widths by dragging headers.
- **Keyboard Shortcuts**: Ctrl + F to search, Enter to add rows, Tab to move cells is great for efficiency.

Beginner Navigation Scenario

- **Example**: In a project sheet, switch to Gantt view to visualize dependencies (arrows link tasks), then back to Grid for edits.
- **Tips**: Use breadcrumbs (top-left path like Home > Workspace > Sheet) to jump levels. For large sheets, freeze headers (View > Freeze Panes).
- **Pitfalls**: Overlooking the sidebar can make finding items hard—star favorites early.

Pro Tip: Take the "Navigate Smartsheet" module in Level 1 Foundations for interactive practice.

Chapter 4: Creating Your First Sheet

Sheets are Smartsheet's foundation. This chapter expands on column types, hierarchy, imports, and examples.

Sheet limitations: Whichever comes first: 20,000 rows, 400 columns, 500,000 cells. In Table view, up to 50,000 rows and 1 million cells.

Understanding Sheets in Smartsheet

A sheet is the core building block in Smartsheet, functioning like a spreadsheet but with enhanced features for collaboration, visualization, and automation. Sheets store data in rows and columns, support multiple views (Grid, Gantt, Card, Calendar), and can be linked to reports, dashboards, forms, and workflows. For beginners, think of a sheet as a flexible table where you can enter data manually, import from other sources, or collect via forms.

Sheets can be blank or based on templates, which pre-populate structures for common use cases like project plans or inventories. Once created, sheets can be shared, automated, and visualized. Performance is key: Keep sheets under limits to avoid slowdowns.

Step-by-Step Creation of a Sheet

Creating a sheet is simple but customizable. Follow these steps for your first sheet:

1. **Start New**: From the Home screen, click the blue "+" button in the left sidebar or "Create" > "Sheet" from the top menu. This opens the Create New Sheet dialog.
2. **Name the Sheet**: Enter a descriptive name (e.g., "Team Task Tracker"). Names can be up to 50 characters and should be unique within your workspace for easy searching.
3. **Choose a Type**:
    - **Blank Sheet**: Starts empty with a default primary column (Text/Number type, labeled "Primary").
    - **Template**: Browse the Solution Center for pre-built options. Search by keyword (e.g., "project management") or category (e.g., Marketing, IT). Select a template to preview its structure, then click "Use Template" to create a copy.
4. **Select Location**: Choose where to save the sheet in your Home folder, a Workspace (for organization), or a Folder within a workspace. Workspaces are like shared folders for grouping related sheets.
5. **Create the Sheet**: Click "Create." The sheet opens in Grid view, ready for data entry.
6. **Add Columns**: Right-click any column header > "Insert Column Left/Right." Or, use the toolbar: Click the column

icon > "Add Column."

    - Name the column (e.g., "Task Name").
    - Set the type (detailed below).
    - Configure properties (e.g., default value, restrictions).

7. **Add Rows**: Click the "+" icon at the bottom-left, or press Enter in the last row. Drag the row number to reorder.
8. **Set Up Hierarchy**: For structured data (e.g., parent tasks with subtasks), indent rows: Right-click row number > "Indent" (or Alt+Shift+Right Arrow). This creates collapsible hierarchies for better organization.
9. **Import Data (If Needed)**: If starting with existing data, go to File > Import > Choose file type (Excel, CSV, Google Sheet, Trello, etc.). Map columns during import to match Smartsheet types. Preview and confirm.
10. **Save and Share**: Changes auto-save, but click the Share button to add collaborators.

[Image Placeholder: Screenshot of Create New Sheet Dialog]

Detailed Column Types

Columns define data structure. Choose types wisely to enable features like formulas, dependencies, or validations. Here's a comprehensive table and explanations:

Default Columns

Primary Column

- **Purpose**: Serves as the row's primary descriptor, uniquely identifying each row.
- **Features**: Defaults to a Text/Number field. Users can rename it but cannot change its type or remove it.
- **Use Case**: Ideal for naming tasks, projects, or items (e.g., "Project Name").

Attachments

- **Purpose**: Allows users to add or view row-level attachments.
- **Features**: Displays an attachment icon when files are added. Can be hidden.
- **Use Case**: Useful for attaching supporting documents (e.g., project plans).

Comments

- **Purpose**: Facilitates row-level discussions or notes.
- **Features**: Displays a comment icon when conversations exist. Can be hidden.
- **Use Case**: Perfect for team feedback (e.g., "Discuss deadline extension").

Proof

- **Purpose**: Enables adding or viewing row-level proofs.
- **Features**: Can be hidden but is part of the default layout.
- **Use Case**: Used for design reviews (e.g., approving a graphic).

Row Action Indicators

- **Purpose**: Displays row-level status indicators and actions.
- **Features**: Shows reminders, locked row icons, or allows update requests. Can be hidden.
- **Use Case**: Manages task statuses (e.g., "Pending approval alert").

Configurable Columns

Text/Number

- **Purpose**: Stores text, numeric values, or both.
- **Features**: Supports text and numeric formatting. Retains leading zeros as text.
- **Use Case**: Suitable for comments or budgets (e.g., "Budget: $5000").

Contact List

- **Purpose**: Manages contact information for assignments.
- **Features**: Accepts names or emails. Supports up to 20 contacts per cell if multiple allowed.
- **Use Case**: Assigns tasks (e.g., "Assigned To: john.doe@company.com").

Date

- **Purpose**: Handles date entries and supports scheduling.
- **Features**: Allows manual entry or calendar selection. Enables dependencies.
- **Use Case**: Tracks deadlines (e.g., "Due Date: 08/15/2025").

Dropdown List

- **Purpose**: Provides a predefined list of selectable values.
- **Features**: Supports single or multiple value selections.
- **Use Case**: Standardizes status tracking (e.g., "Status: Complete").

Checkbox

- **Purpose**: Represents binary or status selections.
- **Features**: Displays as checkbox, flag, or star. Appears after other column data.

- **Use Case**: Marks task completion (e.g., "Completed: [ ]").

Symbols

- **Purpose**: Visually indicates row status with icons.
- **Features**: Offers predefined symbols (e.g., flags) but no custom options.
- **Use Case**: Indicates priority (e.g., "Priority: [Red Flag]").

Auto-Number

- **Purpose**: Generates unique sequential or custom values.
- **Features**: Supports configurable prefixes (e.g., "ID-001").
- **Use Case**: Assigns unique identifiers (e.g., "Invoice #: INV-2025-001").

System Columns

- **Purpose**: Tracks metadata about row creation and modification.
- **Features**: Includes "Created By," "Created Date," etc. Populates automatically.
- **Use Case**: Audits changes (e.g., "Modified By: jane.smith").

Latest Comment

- **Purpose**: Displays the most recent comment.
- **Features**: Updates automatically with new comments.
- **Use Case**: Quick reference for feedback (e.g., "Latest Comment: Approved").

Duration

- **Purpose**: Manages task duration or calculates time spans.
- **Features**: Accepts manual input or calculates from dates.
- **Use Case**: Plans task lengths (e.g., "Duration: 3 days").

Complex Column Types

MULTI_CONTACT_LIST

- **Purpose**: Handles multiple contacts with complex data.
- **Features**: Returns a complex object with level=2 query.
- **Use Case**: Manages teams (e.g., "Team: john.doe@company.com, jane.smith@company.com").

MULTI_PICKLIST

- **Purpose**: Enhances Dropdown List with multiple values.
- **Features**: Requires level=2 query for complex return.
- **Use Case**: Tracks multiple statuses (e.g., "Tags: Urgent, High Priority").

Notes

- **Customization**: Column properties (e.g., descriptions, restrictions) can be edited by Owners or Admins to provide context or enforce data integrity.
- **Limitations**: Default columns cannot be removed, and some configurable types (e.g., Symbols) lack custom options. Primary column type is fixed as Text/Number.
- **Enhancements**: Features like conditional formatting, formulas, and automation are unlocked based on column type, making them integral to advanced workflows.

Adding Hierarchy and Structure

Hierarchy organizes data into parent-child relationships:

- Indent: Drag the row grip (left of row number) or use keyboard shortcuts.
- Collapse/Expand: Click the arrow next to parent rows.
- Rollups: Use formulas like =SUM(CHILDREN()) in parent cells to aggregate child data.
- Levels: Up to 100 levels deep, but keep to 5-10 for usability.

Example: In an "Event Planning" sheet, create a parent row "Venue" with children "Book Hall" and "Confirm Catering."

Importing Data

- Supported Formats: Excel (.xlsx), CSV, Google Sheets, Microsoft Project, Trello, Asana.
- Steps: File > Import > Select file > Map columns (match types) > Import.
- Tips: Clean data first (remove formulas); handle errors like #INVALID DATA TYPE by adjusting types post-import.
- Limitations: 20,000 rows max; attachments/formulas may not import perfectly.

Examples and Best Practices

- **Scenario**: Build an "Event Planning" sheet: Columns for Task (Text), Owner (Contact), Due Date (Date), Status (Dropdown). Rows: Parent "Venue" with indented children.
- **Best Practices**:
    - Start small: 5-10 columns initially.
    - Use templates: "Project with Gantt" for pre-populated timelines.

  - Organize: Group in workspaces/folders; name consistently.
  - Performance: Limit to 20,000 rows/400 columns; archive old data.
  - Security: Lock columns (right-click > Lock) for sensitive info.
- **Advanced Tips for Beginners**: Enable dependencies (Sheet Settings > Project Settings) for auto-dates; add system columns for tracking creation/modification.

Troubleshooting Common Issues

- **Error: #INVALID COLUMN VALUE**: Wrong type (e.g., text in date column). Solution: Change column type via right-click > Edit Column Properties.
- **Slow Loading**: Too many rows/cells. Solution: Split into multiple sheets; use reports to aggregate.
- **Import Fails**: File too large or mismatched types. Solution: Export to CSV first; import in batches.
- **Hierarchy Breaks**: Indenting too deep. Solution: Outdent (Alt+Shift+Left); use filters to view subsets.
- **Pitfalls**: Using text for dates/numbers breaks formulas; overloading with features so start simple.

Pro Tip: Structure with hierarchy for rollups (e.g., parent row sums child durations).

Chapter 5: Formulas, Functions, and Basic Data Magic

Formulas automate calculations. This chapter dives into syntax, common functions, errors, and cross-sheet links. For a detailed guide, see the expanded section below.

Creating Formulas Basics

- **How-To**: Click cell, type =, then function/references. Press Enter to apply. Use @row for current row (e.g., [Column]@row).
- **References**: [Column Name]row (e.g., [Cost]5), ranges ([Cost]1:[Cost]10), or CHILDREN() for hierarchy sums.

Common Functions with Examples

- **SUM/COUNT**: =SUM(CHILDREN()) totals subtasks; =COUNTIF([Status]:[Status], "Done") counts completed.
- **IF**: =IF([% Complete]@row = 1, "Done", "Pending") for conditional status.
- **TODAY/VLOOKUP**: =TODAY() - [Due Date]@row for days overdue; =VLOOKUP([Task ID]@row, {Other Sheet Range}, 2, false) for lookups.
- **MAX/FIND**: =MAX([Date]1:[Date]10) finds latest; =FIND("error", [Description]@row) locates text.

Cross-Sheet References

- Right-click cell > Insert Cross-Sheet Reference > Select sheet/range. Use {Range Name} in formulas for dynamic links.
- **Reference Limits**: 500,000 cross-sheet references (VLOOKUPs/call-ins), 20,000 inbound cell links (single cell link instead of a range), and no limits on information being sent out to other sheets (call-outs).

Error Handling and Tips

- Common Errors: #UNPARSEABLE (syntax issue, e.g., missing quotes); #INVALID DATA TYPE (wrong types);

#DIVIDE BY ZERO (use IFERROR: =IFERROR(1/0, "N/A")).
- **Beginner Tips**: Use formula builder (fx icon) for auto-suggest. Test in a blank column. Avoid circular references (#CIRCULAR REFERENCE).
- **Scenario**: In a budget sheet, =SUMIF([Category]:[Category], "Marketing", [Amount]:[Amount]) totals category spend.
- **Pitfalls**: Mismatched types (e.g., date in number column) cause #INVALID COLUMN VALUE match via column settings.

Pro Tip: Handle errors with IFERROR for clean sheets.

Formulas: A Comprehensive Beginner-to-Advanced User Guide

Formulas in Smartsheet allow you to perform calculations, manipulate text, handle dates, and create logical decisions directly within your sheets. They turn static data into dynamic insights, automating tasks like summing costs, flagging overdue items, or generating status updates. Smartsheet formulas are similar to Excel but optimized for collaboration, with support for cross-sheet references and hierarchy functions.

This guide assumes basic sheet navigation. We'll cover syntax, references, operators, detailed functions by category, advanced topics, and troubleshooting. Start with simple math, then build to complex nested formulas. Practice in a test sheet to avoid disrupting live data.

Formula Basics

Formulas start with = in a cell and can include numbers, text, functions, operators, and references. They recalculate automatically on changes. Use in any column, but match types (e.g., date formulas in date columns).

Syntax Structure

- Basic: =2 + 3 (result: 5)
- With Function: =SUM(1, 2, 3) (result: 6)
- With References: =[Column1]@row * [Column2]@row

References

References allow formulas to use data from other cells, making them dynamic and responsive to changes.

- **Single Cell**: Reference by [Column Name]row, e.g., =[Task Name]1 pulls the value from row 1 of the "Task Name" column.
- **Range**: Use [Column Name]start_row:[Column Name]end_row, e.g., =SUM([Cost]2:[Cost]5) sums rows 2–5 in the "Cost" column.
- **Entire Column**: [Column Name]:[Column Name], e.g., =SUM([Cost]:[Cost]) sums the entire column.
- **@row Shorthand**: References the current row, e.g., =[Status]@row. Ideal for column formulas to avoid hardcoding row numbers.
- **Absolute References**: Add $ to lock a reference, e.g., =$[Fixed Cost]1 doesn't adjust when copied.

Inserting References:

- While typing a formula, click a cell or drag to select a range and Smartsheet inserts the reference automatically.
- For columns with multi-word names or special characters, use square brackets, e.g., [Purchase Cost]2.
- For cross-sheet references (used in VLOOKUP, MATCH, COLLECT), use curly braces {} (detailed in the Lookup section below).

Copying Formulas:

- Drag the fill handle (bottom-right corner of the cell) to copy to adjacent cells and references adjust relative to position.
- Auto-fill: Smartsheet may apply formulas to new rows below if it detects a pattern (e.g., two identical formulas in consecutive rows).
- For cross-sheet references, use the Sheet Reference Manager to avoid broken links when sheets are renamed or moved.

Operators

Operators perform calculations, comparisons, or concatenation.

- **Math Operators**:

- + : Addition
- - : Subtraction

- * : Multiplication
    - / : Division
    - ^ : Exponentiation (e.g., 2^3 = 8)

- **Comparison Operators** (used in logic):
    - < : Less than
    - : Greater than
    - <= : Less than or equal to
    - = : Greater than or equal to
    - = : Equal to
    - <> : Not equal to
- **Concatenation**: Use + to join text, e.g., =[First Name]@row + " " + [Last Name]@row.

Example: =IF([Score]@row >= 80, "Pass", "Fail") uses >= to compare and return text.

Tips for Beginners

- **Start Simple**: Begin with basic math or text formulas before tackling functions.
- **Use the Toolbar**: Click the ∑ (Sum) icon for quick access to common functions like SUM, AVG, MIN, MAX.
- **Function List**: Type = and a letter to see matching functions in the formula bar; hover for descriptions.
- **Escape Characters**: Use backslash () for quotes or brackets in text, e.g., =""Quoted Text"" or =[ColumnNameColumn NameColumnName]@row.
- **Percentages**: Smartsheet uses decimals (0.5 = 50%). Set column format to % for display.
- **Symbols**: For RYG balls, return "Red", "Yellow", "Green"; for checkboxes, return 1 (checked) or 0 (unchecked).
- **Avoid Circular References**: Don't reference the formula's own cell, directly or indirectly.
- **Test Safely**: Use a sandbox sheet to experiment without risking live data.
- **Formula Limits**: Smartsheet supports up to 400,000 cells per sheet and 100,000 incoming cross-sheet reference cells.

Detailed Functions

Smartsheet offers over 100 functions across categories like Numeric, Text, Date, Logical, Lookup, Hierarchy, and Advanced. Below, we cover key functions in each category, with syntax, description, parameters, examples, and practical tips.

Numeric (Math) Functions

These handle calculations, rounding, and conversions.

1. **ABS**
    - **Syntax**: ABS(number)
    - **Description**: Returns the absolute (positive) value of a number, ignoring its sign. This is useful for scenarios where magnitude matters more than direction, such as calculating deviations or distances in datasets.
    - **Parameters**:
        - number: The numeric value to convert, which can be a literal number, cell reference, or result of another formula.
    - **Example**:
        - Formula: =ABS(-15)
        - Result: 15
        - Explanation: Converts a negative number to positive. In practice, this can be used to normalize losses in a profit/loss column.
    - Advanced Scenario: =ABS([Actual Cost]@row - [Budgeted Cost]@row) calculates the absolute difference between actual and budgeted costs, helping identify variances without sign bias.
    - **Tips**:
        - Works with decimal values, e.g., ABS(-3.14159) returns 3.14159.
        - If the input is non-numeric (e.g., text), it returns #INVALID DATA TYPE.
        - Combine with IF for conditional absolutizing, e.g., =IF([Value]@row < 0, ABS([Value]@row), [Value]@row) to only absolute negatives.
        - In financial sheets, use to normalize values for charting or reporting, ensuring all

variances are positive for easier comparison.
      - Performance note: ABS is lightweight and fast, even in large ranges.

2. **AVG**
   - **Syntax**: AVG(number1, [number2, ...])
   - **Description**: Calculates the arithmetic mean (average) of a set of numbers by summing them and dividing by the count of non-blank values. This is essential for summarizing data trends, like average sales or scores.
   - **Parameters**:
      - number1: The first number, range, or cell reference.
      - [number2, ...]: Optional additional numbers or ranges (up to 255 arguments).
   -
   - **Example**:
      - Formula: =AVG(10, 20, 30)
      - Result: 20
      - Explanation: (10 + 20 + 30) / 3 = 20.
   - Advanced Scenario: =AVG([Sales Q1]@row:[Sales Q4]@row) averages quarterly sales in the same row, useful for annual overviews.
   - **Tips**:
      - Ignores text, blanks, and non-numeric values automatically.
      - Use with CHILDREN() for hierarchy averages, e.g., =AVG(CHILDREN([Score]@row)) to average sub-task scores.
      - For weighted averages, combine with SUM and COUNT, e.g.,

=SUM([Value]1:[Value]10 * [Weight]1:[Weight]10) / SUM([Weight]1:[Weight]10).

- In column formulas, pair with IF to exclude outliers, e.g., =AVG(IF([Score]@row > 0, [Score]@row, "")).
- Performance: Efficient for up to thousands of cells; for very large datasets, use Sheet Summary for aggregation.

3. **CEILING**
    - **Syntax**: CEILING(number, [significance])
    - **Description**: Rounds a number up to the nearest multiple of significance, away from zero. This is commonly used in pricing, inventory, or scheduling to round up to standard units.
    - **Parameters**:
        - number: The value to round.
        - [significance]: The multiple to round to (default 1; can be decimal or negative).
    - **Example**:
        - Formula: =CEILING(2.3, 1)
        - Result: 3
        - Explanation: Rounds 2.3 up to the next whole number.
    - Advanced Scenario: =CEILING([Price]@row, 0.05) rounds prices to the nearest nickel, ensuring consistent billing.
    - **Tips**:
        - For negative numbers, rounds away from zero, e.g., CEILING(-2.3, 1) = -3.
        - Negative significance rounds to the left of the decimal, e.g., CEILING(123, -10) =

130.
        - Opposite of FLOOR; use for scenarios where overestimation is preferred (e.g., resource allocation).
        - Combine with INT for custom rounding logic.
        - Avoid in date columns; use WORKDAY for time-based rounding.

4. **COUNT**
    - **Syntax**: COUNT(value1, [value2, ...])
    - **Description**: Counts the number of non-blank cells in a range, including text, numbers, dates, or symbols. This is fundamental for tracking completion rates or inventory counts.
    - **Parameters**:
        - value1: The first value or range.
        - [value2, ...]: Optional additional values or ranges.
    - **Example**:
        - Formula: =COUNT([Task]1:[Task]10)
        - Result: Number of non-blank tasks in rows 1–10.
        - Explanation: Counts any filled cell, regardless of type.
    - Advanced Scenario: =COUNT(CHILDREN()) counts the number of sub-tasks under a parent row in a hierarchical sheet.
    - **Tips**:
        - Use COUNTIF for conditional counting.
        - In multi-select columns, counts the cell if any value is present.
        - Pair with IF to create dashboards, e.g.,

=COUNT(IF([Status]@row = "Complete", 1, "")).

- For entire sheets, use Sheet Summary fields to avoid grid clutter.
- Performance: Handles large ranges well, but combine with filters for efficiency.

5. **FLOOR**
    - **Syntax**: FLOOR(number, [significance])
    - **Description**: Rounds a number down to the nearest multiple of significance, toward zero. Useful for conservative estimates, like flooring hours in time tracking.
    - **Parameters**: Same as CEILING.
    - **Example**:
        - Formula: =FLOOR(2.7, 1)
        - Result: 2
        - Explanation: Rounds 2.7 down to the nearest whole number.
    - Advanced Scenario: =FLOOR([Hours Worked]@row, 0.25) rounds time to the nearest lower quarter-hour for billing.
    - **Tips**:
        - For negative numbers, rounds toward zero, e.g., FLOOR(-2.7, 1) = -2.
        - Negative significance for tens/hundreds, e.g., FLOOR(123, -10) = 120.
        - Opposite of CEILING; use when underestimation is safer (e.g., stock levels).
        - Combine with MOD to get fractional parts.
6. **INT**
    - **Syntax**: INT(number)

- **Description**: Returns the integer part of a number by truncating the decimal portion toward zero. Ideal for extracting whole numbers from decimals, like days from time durations.
- **Parameters**:
  - number: The value to truncate.
- **Example**:
  - Formula: =INT(5.9)
  - Result: 5
  - Explanation: Discards the 0.9 fractional part.
- Advanced Scenario: =INT([Total Days]@row) extracts whole days from a duration calculation.
- **Tips**:
  - For negative numbers, truncates toward zero, e.g., INT(-5.9) = -5.
  - Use with MOD to separate integer and fractional parts, e.g., =MOD([Number]@row, 1) for decimals.
  - Differs from FLOOR for negatives; choose based on rounding needs.

7. **LARGE**
   - **Syntax**: LARGE(range, k)
   - **Description**: Returns the k-the largest value in a range, useful for rankings or top performer analysis.
   - **Parameters**:
     - range: The data set to evaluate.
     - k: The position from the largest (1 = largest, 2 = second-largest, etc.).
   - **Example**:
     - Formula: =LARGE([Scores]1:[Scores]5, 2)

        - Result: The second-highest score in the range.
        - Explanation: Sorts the range internally and picks the k.
    - Advanced Scenario: =LARGE(CHILDREN([Sales]@row), 1) finds the top sales value among sub-items.
    - **Tips**:
        - Errors if k is larger than the range size or negative (#INVALID VALUE).
        - Use with INDEX for advanced lookups, e.g., finding the name associated with the largest value.
        - For ties, returns the first occurrence.

8. **MAX**
    - **Syntax**: MAX(value1, [value2, ...])
    - **Description**: Returns the maximum value in a set, working with numbers or dates (latest date).
    - **Parameters**:
        - value1: First value or range.
        - [value2, ...]: Optional additional.
    - **Example**:
        - Formula: =MAX(5, 10, 8)
        - Result: 10
        - Explanation: Identifies the highest number.
    - Advanced Scenario: =MAX([Due Date]:[Due Date]) finds the latest due date in a column.
    - **Tips**:
        - Ignores text and blanks; treats dates as numbers.
        - Use with CHILDREN for hierarchy max, e.g., =MAX(CHILDREN([End

Date]@row)).
        - For conditional max, use MAX(COLLECT(...)).

9. **MEDIAN**
    - **Syntax**: MEDIAN(number1, [number2, ...])
    - **Description**: Returns the median (middle value) in a sorted set of numbers, robust to outliers.
    - **Parameters**: Same as AVG.
    - **Example**:
        - Formula: =MEDIAN(1, 3, 5)
        - Result: 3
        - Explanation: Middle value; for even count, averages the two middle numbers.
    - Advanced Scenario: =MEDIAN([Salaries]1:[Salaries]100) finds the median salary.
    - **Tips**:
        - Sorts internally; ignores non-numbers.
        - Useful in statistics for central tendency without average's outlier sensitivity.

10. **MIN**
    - **Syntax**: MIN(value1, [value2, ...])
    - **Description**: Returns the minimum value (lowest number or earliest date).
    - **Parameters**: Same as MAX.
    - **Example**:
        - Formula: =MIN(5, 10, 8)
        - Result: 5
        - Explanation: Identifies the lowest value.
    - Advanced Scenario: =MIN([Start Date]:[Start Date]) finds the earliest start date.

- **Tips**:
    - Ignores text; use with dates for timelines.
    - Conditional min: MIN(COLLECT(...)).

1. **MOD**
    - **Syntax**: MOD(dividend, divisor)
    - **Description**: Returns the remainder after division, useful for cycles, grouping, or remainders.
    - **Parameters**:
        - dividend: Number to divide.
        - divisor: Number to divide by (cannot be 0).
    - **Example**:
        - Formula: =MOD(10, 3)
        - Result: 1
        - Explanation: 10 / 3 = 3 with remainder 1.
    - Advanced Scenario: =MOD([Total Items]@row, 5) determines batches of 5.
    - **Tips**:
        - Errors on divide by zero (#DIVIDE BY ZERO).
        - For negative dividends, remainder sign matches divisor.
        - Use for even/odd checks, e.g., =IF(MOD([Number]@row, 2) = 0, "Even", "Odd").
2. **SUM**
    - **Syntax**: SUM(value1, [value2, ...])
    - **Description**: Adds up a set of numbers, foundational for totals and aggregations.
    - **Parameters**: Same as AVG.
    - **Example**:
        - Formula: =SUM(1, 2, 3)

        - Result: 6
        - Explanation: Basic addition.
    - Advanced Scenario: =SUM([Expenses]1:[Expenses]10) totals expenses.
    - **Tips**:
        - Ignores text and blanks.
        - Use SUMIF/SUMIFS for conditions.
        - In hierarchies, =SUM(CHILDREN()) for sub-total roll-ups.

Text Functions

These manipulate strings for formatting, extraction, and transformation.

1. **CHAR**
    - **Syntax**: CHAR(number)
    - **Description**: Returns the character corresponding to an ASCII code, useful for inserting special characters or line breaks.
    - **Parameters**:
        - number: ASCII code (1–255).
    - **Example**:
        - Formula: =CHAR(65)
        - Result: "A"
        - Explanation: ASCII 65 is "A".
    - Advanced Scenario: = [Name]@row + CHAR(10) + [Address]@row inserts a line break for multi-line cells.
    - **Tips**:
        - Common codes: 10 (line break), 32 (space), 34 (quote).
        - Use in concatenation for formatting.

2. **CONCATENATE**
    - **Syntax**: CONCATENATE(value1, [value2, ...])
    - **Description**: Joins multiple values into a single string, with no automatic separator.
    - **Parameters**:
        - value1: First value (text, number, or reference).
        - [value2, ...]: Additional values.
    - **Example**:
        - Formula: =CONCATENATE("Hello", " ", "World")
        - Result: "Hello World"
        - Explanation: Combines strings; add spaces manually.
    - Advanced Scenario: =CONCATENATE([First Name]@row, " ", [Last Name]@row) creates full names.
    - **Tips**:
        - Equivalent to using + for concatenation.
        - Numbers are converted to text automatically.
        - Use for dynamic labels or IDs.
3. **FIND**
    - **Syntax**: FIND(search_for, text_to_search, [start_position])
    - **Description**: Returns the starting position (1-based) of a substring within text; returns 0 if not found. Case-sensitive.
    - **Parameters**:
        - search_for: The string to find.
        - text_to_search: The text to search in.
        - [start_position]: Optional starting point

(default 1).

- **Example**:
  - Formula: =FIND("cat", "concatenate")
  - Result: 4
  - Explanation: "cat" starts at position 4.
- Advanced Scenario: =FIND("@", [Email]@row) finds the position of the @ in an email to extract domains.
- **Tips**:
  - Combine with MID or LEFT for substring extraction, e.g., =MID([Text]@row, FIND(":", [Text]@row) + 1, LEN([Text]@row)).
  - For case-insensitive, use LOWER on both strings.

4. **LEFT**
   - **Syntax**: LEFT(text, [num_chars])
   - **Description**: Extracts the leftmost characters from a string.
   - **Parameters**:
     - text: The string to extract from.
     - [num_chars]: Number of characters (default: all).
   - **Example**:
     - Formula: =LEFT("Smartsheet", 5)
     - Result: "Smart"
     - Explanation: First 5 characters.
   - Advanced Scenario: =LEFT([Product Code]@row, 3) extracts a prefix.
   - **Tips**:
     - If num_chars exceeds length, returns the whole string.

        - Use with FIND to extract up to a delimiter.

5. **LEN**
    - **Syntax**: LEN(text)
    - **Description**: Returns the length of a string, including spaces, useful for validation or formatting.
    - **Parameters**:
        - text: The string.

- **Example**:
    - Formula: =LEN("Hello World")
    - Result: 11
    - Explanation: Counts all characters.
- Advanced Scenario: =IF(LEN([Description]@row) > 100, "Too Long", "OK") validates length.
- **Tips**:
    - Numbers are converted to text for counting.
    - Use in IF for data quality checks.

1. **LOWER**
    - **Syntax**: LOWER(text)
    - **Description**: Converts text to lowercase, standardizing for comparisons or lookups.
    - **Parameters**:
        - text: The string.
    - **Example**:
        - Formula: =LOWER("SMARTSheet")
        - Result: "smartsheet"
        - Explanation: All lowercase.
    - Advanced Scenario: =VLOOKUP(LOWER([Search]@row), {Lookup Table}, 2) for case-insensitive lookups.
    - **Tips**:

        - Non-letter characters remain unchanged.

2. **MID**
    - **Syntax**: MID(text, start_num, num_chars)
    - **Description**: Extracts a substring from the middle of text.

- **Parameters**:
    - text: The string.
    - start_num: Starting position (1-based).
    - num_chars: Length to extract.
- **Example**:
    - Formula: =MID("Smartsheet", 6, 5)
    - Result: "sheet"
    - Explanation: Starts at position 6, extracts 5 characters.
- Advanced Scenario: =MID([Full Code]@row, FIND("-", [Full Code]@row) + 1, 4) extracts after a dash.
- **Tips**:
    - If start_num + num_chars exceeds length, returns up to the end.
    - Combine with FIND for dynamic extraction.

1. **REPLACE**
    - **Syntax**: REPLACE(text, start_num, num_chars, new_text)
    - **Description**: Replaces a specific portion of text with new text.
    - **Parameters**:
        - text: Original string.
        - start_num: Start position.
        - num_chars: Length to replace.
        - new_text: Replacement string.

- **Example**:
  - Formula: =REPLACE("2024 Report", 1, 4, "2025")
  - Result: "2025 Report"
  - Explanation: Replaces the first 4 characters.
- Advanced Scenario: =REPLACE([Phone]@row, 1, 3, "***") masks area code.
- **Tips**:
  - For full replacements, use SUBSTITUTE.
  - Can insert by replacing 0 characters.

2. **RIGHT**
   - **Syntax**: RIGHT(text, [num_chars])
   - **Description**: Extracts the rightmost characters from a string.
   - **Parameters**: Same as LEFT.
   - **Example**:
     - Formula: =RIGHT("Smartsheet", 5)
     - Result: "sheet"
     - Explanation: Last 5 characters.
   - Advanced Scenario: =RIGHT([File Name]@row, 3) extracts file extension.
   - **Tips**:
     - Similar to LEFT; use for suffixes.
3. **SUBSTITUTE**
   - **Syntax**: SUBSTITUTE(text, old_text, new_text, [instance_num])
   - **Description**: Replaces occurrences of old text with new text; optional to specify which instance.
   - **Parameters**:
     - text: Original string.
     - old_text: Text to replace.
     - new_text: Replacement.

        - [instance_num]: Specific occurrence (default: all).
    - **Example**:
        - Formula: =SUBSTITUTE("cat dog cat", "cat", "bird")
        - Result: "bird dog bird"
        - Explanation: Replaces all "cat".
    - Advanced Scenario: =SUBSTITUTE([Text]@row, "old", "new", 1) replaces only the first occurrence.
    - **Tips**:
        - Case-sensitive; use LOWER for insensitivity.
        - Useful for cleaning data, e.g., removing commas.

1. **UPPER**
    - **Syntax**: UPPER(text)
    - **Description**: Converts text to uppercase.
    - **Parameters**: The string.
    - **Example**:
        - Formula: =UPPER("smartsheet")
        - Result: "SMARTSHEET"
        - Explanation: All uppercase.
    - Advanced Scenario: For standardized codes or acronyms.

Date Functions

These handle date calculations, extraction, and manipulation.

1. **DATE**
    - **Syntax**: DATE(year, month, day)
    - **Description**: Creates a valid date from year, month,

and day components, validating for leap years and month lengths.

- **Parameters**:
  - year: Four-digit year (e.g., 2025).
  - month: 1–12.
  - day: 1–31 (depending on month).
- **Example**:
  - Formula: =DATE(2025, 8, 3)
  - Result: 08/03/2025 (format depends on regional settings).
  - Explanation: Constructs a date.
- Advanced Scenario: =DATE(YEAR(TODAY()), MONTH(TODAY()), 1) returns the first day of the current month.
- **Tips**:
  - Errors on invalid dates (e.g., DATE(2025, 2, 30) = #INVALID VALUE).
  - Use in date columns; combine with TODAY for relative dates.

2. **DATEONLY**
   - **Syntax**: DATEONLY(date)
   - **Description**: Extracts the date portion from a datetime value, stripping time.
   - **Parameters**:
     - date: A date or datetime value.
   - **Example**:
     - Formula: =DATEONLY("08/03/2025 12:00 PM")
     - Result: 08/03/2025
     - Explanation: Removes time component.
   - Advanced Scenario: Useful for cell links from forms or integrations that include timestamps.

- **Tips**:
    - Ideal for normalizing dates from external sources.
    - Returns #DATE EXPECTED if input isn't a date.

3. **DAY**
    - **Syntax**: DAY(date)
    - **Description**: Extracts the day of the month (1–31).
    - **Parameters**:
        - date: A date value.
    - **Example**:
        - Formula: =DAY(TODAY())
        - Result: Current day (e.g., 3).
    - Advanced Scenario: =IF(DAY([Due Date]@row) = 1, "Start of Month", "").
    - **Tips**:
        - Use with MONTH and YEAR for date reconstruction.
4. **MONTH**
    - **Syntax**: MONTH(date)
    - **Description**: Extracts the month (1–12).
    - **Parameters**: A date value.
    - **Example**:
        - Formula: =MONTH("08/03/2025")
        - Result: 8
    - Advanced Scenario: = "Q" + INT((MONTH([Date]@row) + 2)/3) calculates quarter.
    - **Tips**:
        - For month names, nest in TEXT or use IF chains.
5. **NETDAYS**

- **Syntax**: NETDAYS(start_date, end_date)
- **Description**: Calculates the total number of days between two dates, inclusive.
- **Parameters**:
    - start_date: Starting date.
    - end_date: Ending date.
- **Example**:
    - Formula: =NETDAYS([Start]@row, [End]@row)
    - Result: Number of days, including weekends.
- Advanced Scenario: =NETDAYS(TODAY(), [Due Date]@row) for days remaining.
- **Tips**:
    - If start > end, returns negative.
    - Use NETWORKDAYS for business days.

1. **TODAY**
    - **Syntax**: TODAY([number])
    - **Description**: Returns the current date, optionally offset by a number of days.
    - **Parameters**:
        - [number]: Days to add (positive) or subtract (negative; default 0).
    - **Example**:
        - Formula: =TODAY()
        - Result: Current date (e.g., 08/03/2025).
        - Explanation: Updates automatically daily.
    - Advanced Scenario: =IF([Due Date]@row < TODAY(), "Overdue", "On Time") for status flags.
    - **Tips**:
        - Sheets with TODAY recalculate daily

when opened.
        - Use TODAY(-30) for 30 days ago.

2. **WEEKDAY**
    - **Syntax**: WEEKDAY(date)
    - **Description**: Returns the day of the week (1 = Sunday, 7 = Saturday).
    - **Parameters**: A date value.
    - **Example**:
        - Formula: =WEEKDAY(TODAY())
        - Result: Current weekday number.
    - Advanced Scenario: =IF(WEEKDAY([Date]@row) = 1, "Weekend", "Weekday").
    - **Tips**:
        - Use for scheduling or filters.
3. **WORKDAY**
    - **Syntax**: WORKDAY(start_date, num_days, [holidays])
    - **Description**: Adds a number of workdays to a start date, excluding weekends and optional holidays.
    - **Parameters**:
        - start_date: Base date.
        - num_days: Workdays to add (negative to subtract).
        - [holidays]: Range of holiday dates to exclude.
    - **Example**:
        - Formula: =WORKDAY(TODAY(), 5)
        - Result: 5 workdays ahead.
    - Advanced Scenario: =WORKDAY([Start]@row, [Duration]@row, {Holiday List}) calculates end date excluding holidays.

- **Tips**:
    - Holidays must be a range or cross-sheet reference.
    - Use for project timelines.

4. **YEAR**
    - **Syntax**: YEAR(date)
    - **Description**: Extracts the year from a date.
    - **Parameters**: A date value.
    - **Example**:
        - Formula: =YEAR(TODAY())
        - Result: 2025
    - Advanced Scenario: =IF(YEAR([Date]@row) = YEAR(TODAY()), "Current Year", "Archive").

Logical Functions

These enable decision-making and conditional logic.

1. **AND**
    - **Syntax**: AND(logical1, logical2, ...)
    - **Description**: Returns TRUE if all conditions are true; FALSE otherwise. Useful for multi-condition checks.
    - **Parameters**:
        - logical1: First condition (e.g., [Score]@row > 80).
        - logical2, ...: Additional conditions (up to 255).
    - **Example**:
        - Formula: =AND([Score]@row > 80, [Attendance]@row = "Yes")
        - Result: TRUE if both are true.
        - Explanation: All must be true.

- Advanced Scenario: =IF(AND([Status]@row = "Complete", [Approved]@row = 1), "Ready", "Pending") checks multiple statuses.
- **Tips**:
  - Nest in IF for complex logic.
  - Conditions can be formulas or comparisons.

2. **IF**
   - **Syntax**: IF(logical_test, value_if_true, [value_if_false])
   - **Description**: Evaluates a condition and returns one value if true, another if false. Core for conditional outputs.
   - **Parameters**:
     - logical_test: The condition to test.
     - value_if_true: Result if true.
     - [value_if_false]: Result if false (default blank).
   - **Example**:
     - Formula: =IF([Status]@row = "Complete", "Green", "Red")
     - Result: "Green" or "Red" for RYG symbols.
     - Explanation: Automates status indicators.
   - Advanced Scenario: Nested IF for grades: =IF([Score]@row > 90, "A", IF([Score]@row > 80, "B", IF([Score]@row > 70, "C", "F"))).
   - **Tips**:
     - Nest up to 7 levels for multi-tier logic.
     - Return symbols, text, or numbers.
     - Use for error handling, e.g., =IF([Denom]@row <> 0, [Num]@row / [Denom]@row, "N/A").

3. **IFERROR**
    - **Syntax**: IFERROR(value, value_if_error)
    - **Description**: Returns an alternative value if the expression results in an error.
    - **Parameters**:
        - value: The expression to evaluate.
        - value_if_error: Result if error occurs.
    - **Example**:
        - Formula: =IFERROR(1/0, "Error")
        - Result: "Error"
        - Explanation: Catches #DIVIDE BY ZERO.
    - Advanced Scenario: =IFERROR(VLOOKUP([ID]@row, {Table}, 2), "Not Found") handles missing lookups.
    - **Tips**:
        - Wrap risky formulas to maintain clean sheets.
        - Doesn't catch all errors (e.g., circular references).
4. **ISBLANK**
    - **Syntax**: ISBLANK(value)
    - **Description**: Returns TRUE if the cell is blank or empty.
    - **Parameters**:
        - value: The cell or expression to check.
    - **Example**:
        - Formula: =IF(ISBLANK([Name]@row), "Enter Name", [Name]@row)
        - Result: Prompts if blank.
    - Advanced Scenario: =COUNTIF([Column]:[Column],

ISBLANK(@cell)) counts blanks in a column.

- **Tips**:
    - Use @cell in range functions for cell-by-cell checks.

5. **NOT**
    - **Syntax**: NOT(logical)
    - **Description**: Reverses a logical value (TRUE to FALSE, and vice versa).
    - **Parameters**:
        - logical: The condition to reverse.
    - **Example**:
        - Formula: =NOT([Done]@row = 1)
        - Result: TRUE if not done.
    - Advanced Scenario: =IF(NOT(ISBLANK([Field]@row)), "Filled", "Empty").
    - **Tips**:
        - Useful for inverting conditions in IF or AND/OR.

1. **OR**
    - **Syntax**: OR(logical1, logical2, ...)
    - **Description**: Returns TRUE if any condition is true.
    - **Parameters**:
        - logical1: First condition.
        -
    - **Example**:
        - Formula: =OR([Priority]@row = "High", [Status]@row = "Delayed")
        - Result: TRUE if either is true.
    - Advanced Scenario: =IF(OR([Region]@row =

"East", [Region]@row = "West"), "Coastal", "Inland").

- **Tips**:
    - Combine with AND for complex logic.

Lookup and Reference Functions

These functions are powerful for data retrieval, filtering, and aggregation, often involving references to ranges within the same sheet or across sheets.

Adding references, particularly cross-sheet ones, is crucial for these functions to work beyond the current sheet. Cross-sheet references use curly braces {} and are managed to avoid performance issues or broken links. Here's a deep dive on how to add them:

Step-by-Step Guide to Adding References for Lookup, MATCH, or COLLECT Functions:

1. **Identify the Source Data**:
    - Determine if the reference is in the same sheet (use [Column]row syntax) or another sheet (cross-sheet).
    - For cross-sheet, open the source sheet and note the range (e.g., an entire column or specific rows).
2. **Enter the Formula and Trigger Reference Creation**:
    - Start typing the formula in the target cell, e.g., =VLOOKUP([Search Key]@row, .
    - When you need the range, type { to open the Reference Another Sheet dialog.
    - Alternatively, click the "Reference Another Sheet" link in the formula bar.
3. **Create or Select the Reference**:
    - In the dialog, search for the source sheet by name.
    - Select the sheet, then highlight the range (click a cell

   for single, drag for range, or click column header for entire column).
   - Name the reference descriptively (e.g., "Employee Table Range") for easy management.
   - Click "Insert Reference"—Smartsheet inserts {Reference Name} (e.g., {Employee Table Range}).
   - The reference is now saved in the Sheet Reference Manager (access via Account > Sheet Reference Manager).
4. **Complete the Formula**:
   - Continue typing, e.g., =VLOOKUP([Search Key]@row, {Employee Table Range}, 3, FALSE).
   - Test by entering values; if #INVALID REF appears, check the manager for broken refs.
5. **Manage and Troubleshoot References**:
   - Limit: 100 unique cross-sheet references per sheet; 100,000 incoming cells total.
   - Edit/Delete: In Sheet Reference Manager, update ranges or delete unused ones.
   - Performance: Minimize large ranges; use specific rows where possible.
   - Sharing: References work if the user has access to the source sheet.
   - Best Practice: Use entire columns for dynamic ranges, e.g., {Source Sheet Column Name:Column Name}.
6. **Advanced Tips for References**:
   - Dynamic Ranges: Use INDIRECT for variable refs, but note it's limited.
   - Error Handling: Wrap in IFERROR, e.g., =IFERROR(VLOOKUP(...), "No Match").
   - Optimization: For frequent lookups, consider

DataMesh or Index/Match combo for flexibility.
- Security: References respect sharing permissions; unlicensed users see #BLOCKED.
- Bulk Creation: Copy formulas with refs—they carry over, but verify in manager.

Now, let's detail the functions.

1. **COLLECT**
   - **Syntax**: COLLECT(range, criterion_range1, criterion1, [criterion_range2, criterion2, ...])
   - **Description**: Returns a filtered range of values from range that meet all specified criteria. It's a building block for advanced aggregations like SUMIFS or COUNTIFS, allowing multi-criteria filtering before applying other functions. Unlike VLOOKUP, it's not for single lookups but for collecting subsets of data.
   - **Parameters**:
     - range: The data to return (e.g., sales values).
     - criterion_range1: The range to test against criterion1.
     - criterion1: The condition (e.g., "West" or >100).
     - [criterion_range2, criterion2, ...]: Additional pairs (up to 100).
   - **Example**:
     - Formula: =SUM(COLLECT([Sales]:[Sales], [Region]:[Region], "West"))
     - Result: Sum of sales where region is "West".
     - Explanation: COLLECT filters [Sales] to

only rows where [Region] = "West", then SUM aggregates.

- Advanced Scenario: Cross-sheet multi-criteria: =AVERAGE(COLLECT({Remote Sales Range}, {Remote Region Range}, "West", {Remote Year Range}, 2025)) averages sales for West in 2025 from another sheet.
- **Tips**:
    - All criterion ranges must be the same size as range or errors occur (#INCORRECT ARGUMENT SET).
    - Use operators in criteria, e.g., ">100" or "<>Blank".
    - For blanks, use "" as criterion.
    - Combine with AVG, MAX, JOIN, etc., for powerful summaries.
    - Performance: Efficient for filters; use in Sheet Summary for dashboard metrics.
    - Adding References for COLLECT: Follow the step-by-step above; for multiple ranges, create separate refs (e.g., {Sales}, {Region}). Ensure refs align in row count.

2. **COUNTIF**
    - **Syntax**: COUNTIF(range, criterion)
    - **Description**: Counts cells in a range that meet a single criterion.
    - **Parameters**:
        - range: The range to count.
        - criterion: The condition.
    - **Example**:
        - Formula: =COUNTIF([Status]:[Status], "Complete")

        - Result: Number of "Complete" statuses.
    - Advanced Scenario: =COUNTIF({Remote Tasks}, "High Priority") counts from another sheet.
3. **COUNTIFS**
    - **Syntax**: COUNTIFS(range1, criterion1, [range2, criterion2, ...])
    - **Description**: Counts cells meeting multiple criteria.
    - **Parameters**: Paired ranges and criteria.
    - **Example**:
        - Formula: =COUNTIFS([Status]:[Status], "Complete", [Priority]:[Priority], "High")
        - Result: Count of high-priority completes.
    - Advanced Scenario: Cross-sheet: =COUNTIFS({Remote Status}, "Complete", {Remote Priority}, "High").
4. **HAS**
    - **Syntax**: HAS(range, criterion)
    - **Description**: Returns TRUE if a multi-select or multi-contact cell contains the exact criterion.
    - **Parameters**:
        - range: Cell or range (often @row for single).
        - criterion: Exact value to check for.
    - **Example**:
        - Formula: =HAS([Team]@row, "John Doe")
        - Result: TRUE if "John Doe" is in the multi-contact list.
        - Explanation: Exact match, ignoring order.
    - Advanced Scenario: =IF(HAS([Tags]@row, "Urgent"), "Priority", "Normal").
    - **Tips**:

   - Case-sensitive; for multi-select dropdowns.
   - Use in filters or IF for tagging.

5. **INDEX**
   - **Syntax**: INDEX(range, row_index, [column_index])
   - **Description**: Returns the value at a specified position in a range.
   - **Parameters**:
     - range: The data range (single or multi-column).
     - row_index: Row position (1-based).
     - [column_index]: Column position (default 1).
   - **Example**:
     - Formula: =INDEX([Names]1:[Names]10, 3)
     - Result: Value in row 3 of the range.
   - Advanced Scenario: Combined with MATCH: =INDEX([Data]1:[Data]10, MATCH("Key", [Keys]1:[Keys]10, 0)) for flexible lookups.
   - **Tips**:
     - Preferred over VLOOKUP for left-lookups or performance.
     - Adding References: Use {Range} for cross-sheet; ensure range includes rows/columns needed.
6. **MATCH**
   - **Syntax**: MATCH(search_value, range, [search_type])
   - **Description**: Returns the 1-based position of a value within a range. It's often nested with INDEX for lookups, providing more flexibility than

VLOOKUP since it can search any column and return positions for further use.

- **Parameters**:
  - search_value: The value to find.
  - range: The range to search (single column recommended).
  - [search_type]: 0 for exact match (default), 1 for largest <= (ascending sort), -1 for smallest >= (descending sort).
- **Example**:
  - Formula: =MATCH("Apple", [Fruits]1:[Fruits]5, 0)
  - Result: Position of "Apple" (e.g., 2).
  - Explanation: Searches for exact "Apple".
- Advanced Scenario: Cross-sheet lookup position: =MATCH([ID]@row, {Employee IDs Range}, 0) returns row number of matching ID.
- **Tips**:
  - Returns #NO MATCH if not found; wrap in IFERROR.
  - For sorted ranges, use 1 or -1 for approximate matches (faster but requires sorting).
  - Case-insensitive for text; use LOWER if needed.
  - Performance: Faster than VLOOKUP for large datasets when combined with INDEX.
  - Adding References for MATCH:
    - Step 1: Identify the search range in the source sheet (e.g., a column of IDs).

- Step 2: In the formula, after MATCH(value, , type { to open the dialog.
- Step 3: Select the source sheet, highlight the range (e.g., [ID]:[ID] for entire column), name it (e.g., "ID Lookup Range"), and insert.
- Step 4: Complete with search_type, e.g., =MATCH([Local ID]@row, {ID Lookup Range}, 0).
- Step 5: If using with INDEX, create a separate ref for the return range, ensuring same row count.
- Troubleshooting: If ranges don't align (e.g., different sheets), verify in manager; test with small ranges first.
- Advanced: For 2D matches, nest MATCH in INDEX, e.g., =INDEX({Data Table}, MATCH(row_key, {Row Keys}, 0), MATCH(column_key, {Column Headers}, 0)) for table lookups.

7. **SUMIF**
   - **Syntax**: SUMIF(range, criterion, [sum_range])
   - **Description**: Sums values in sum_range where range meets criterion.
   - **Parameters**:
     - range: Test range.

        - criterion: Condition.
        - [sum_range]: Optional sum area (default range).
    - **Example**:
        - Formula: =SUMIF([Region]:[Region], "West", [Sales]:[Sales])
        - Result: Sum of West sales.

8. **SUMIFS**
    - **Syntax**: SUMIFS(sum_range, criterion_range1, criterion1, [criterion_range2, criterion2, ...])
    - **Description**: Sums with multiple criteria.
    - **Parameters:** Sum range first, then paired criteria.
    - **Example**:
        - Formula: =SUMIFS([Sales]:[Sales], [Region]:[Region], "West", [Year]:[Year], 2025)
        - Result: Sum for West in 2025.
    - Advanced Scenario: =SUMIFS({Remote Sales}, {Remote Region}, "West", {Remote Year}, YEAR(TODAY())).
9. **VLOOKUP**
    - **Syntax**: VLOOKUP(search_value, lookup_range, column_num, [match_type])
    - **Description**: Searches for a value in the first column of a range and returns a value from the specified column in the same row. It's great for simple table lookups but less flexible than INDEX/MATCH for non-left columns or reverse lookups.
    - **Parameters**:
        - search_value: The value to search for.
        - lookup_range: The table range (first column is searched).

- column_num: The column to return (1-based, from the range's left).
- [match_type]: FALSE for exact (default), TRUE for approximate (sorted range).

- **Example**:
    - Formula: =VLOOKUP("EMP001", [ID]1:[Name]10, 2, FALSE)
    - Result: Name matching "EMP001" from column 2.
    - Explanation: Searches ID column, returns from Name.
- Advanced Scenario: Cross-sheet: =VLOOKUP([Local ID]@row, {Employee Table Range}, 3, FALSE) returns salary from column 3.
- **Tips**:
    - Returns #NO MATCH if not found; use IFERROR.
    - Range must include search column as first.
    - For approximate, sort ascending; use TRUE for performance in large sorted lists.
    - Limitations: Can't look left; use INDEX/MATCH instead.
    - Performance: Slower for very large ranges; limit to necessary columns.
    - Adding References for VLOOKUP:
        - Step 1: Define the lookup table in the source sheet (e.g., columns ID, Name, Salary).
        - Step 2: In the formula, after VLOOKUP(value, , type { to create ref.
        - Step 3: Select sheet, drag over the

table range (e.g., [ID]1:[Salary]100), name it (e.g., "Employee Lookup Table"), insert.

- Step 4: Specify column_num based on the ref's structure (e.g., 1=ID, 2=Name, 3=Salary).
- Step 5: Add match_type; test with known values. If #NO MATCH, check case/spelling or use LOWER.
- Step 6: Manage: If source range changes, edit in Reference Manager to update without breaking formulas.
- Advanced: For dynamic column_num, use MATCH on headers, e.g., =VLOOKUP([ID]@row, {Table}, MATCH("Salary", {Headers}, 0), FALSE).
- Troubleshooting: Ensure ref includes all needed columns; if sheet renamed, refs auto-update but verify.

Hierarchy Functions

For sheets with indentation (parent-child relationships).

1. **ANCESTORS**
   - **Syntax**: ANCESTORS([column_name]@row)
   - **Description**: Returns a range of all ancestor (parent and above) values in the specified column.

- **Parameters**:
    - [column_name]@row: Optional column (default current).
- **Example**:
    - Formula: =JOIN(ANCESTORS([Task Name]@row), " > ")
    - Result: Breadcrumb path like "Project > Phase > Task".
- **Tips**:
    - Use in reports for context.

2. **CHILDREN**
    - **Syntax**: CHILDREN([column_name]@row)
    - **Description**: Returns a range of immediate child values.
    - **Parameters**: Optional column.
    - **Example**:
        - Formula: =SUM(CHILDREN([Cost]@row))
        - Result: Total cost of sub-tasks.
    - **Tips**:
        - In parent rows for roll-ups.
3. **DESCENDANTS**
    - **Syntax**: DESCENDANTS([column_name]@row)
    - **Description**: Returns all descendant values (children and below).
    - **Parameters**: Optional column.
    - **Example**:
        - Formula: =COUNT(DESCENDANTS())
        - Result: Total sub-items count.
    - **Tips**:
        - For deep hierarchies.

4. **PARENT**
    - **Syntax**: PARENT([column_name]@row)
    - **Description**: Returns the immediate parent value.
    - **Parameters**: Optional column.
    - **Example**:
        - Formula: =PARENT([Task Name]@row)
        - Result: Parent task name.
    - **Tips**:
        - Use for upward references.

Advanced Functions

Complex operations for specialized needs.

1. **JOIN**
    - **Syntax**: JOIN(range, [delimiter])
    - **Description**: Combines a range into a single string with an optional delimiter.
    - **Parameters**:
        - range: Values to join.
        - [delimiter]: Separator (default none).
    - **Example**:
        - Formula: =JOIN([Tags]@row, ", ")
        - Result: "Tag1, Tag2".
    - **Tips**:
        - Use with COLLECT for filtered joins.
2. **NETWORKDAYS**
    - **Syntax**: NETWORKDAYS(start_date, end_date, [holidays])
    - **Description**: Calculates business days between dates, excluding weekends and holidays.
    - **Parameters**: Start/end dates, optional holidays range.

- **Example**:
    - Formula: =NETWORKDAYS([Start]@row, [End]@row)
    - Result: Workdays count.
- **Tips**:
    - Negative if start > end.

3. **VALUE**
    - **Syntax**: VALUE(text)
    - **Description**: Converts text to a number.
    - **Parameters**:
        - text: String representing a number.
    - **Example**:
        - Formula: =VALUE("123")
        - Result: 123
    - **Tips**:
        - Use to fix text-imported numbers.

Advanced Topics

Nested Formulas

Nest functions for complexity, e.g., =IF(SUM([Q1]:[Q4]) > 1000, "Target Met", "Below Target").

For multi-conditions: =IF([Score]@row >= 90, "A", IF([Score]@row >= 80, "B", "C")).

Limit nesting to 7 levels; use helper columns for readability.

Array-Like Operations

COLLECT returns filtered ranges for SUM, AVG, etc., acting like arrays.

Cross-Sheet Formulas

Use {} refs; manage in Sheet Reference Manager. Limits: 100 refs/sheet, 100,000 cells.

Column Formulas vs. Cell Formulas

Column formulas are uniform, non-overridable; use for standards.

Using Formulas with Other Features

- Automations: Trigger on formula changes.
- Dashboards: Chart formula results.
- Forms: Pre-populate (not submitted).

Troubleshooting Guide

Common errors, causes, resolutions:

1. **#BLOCKED**
    - Cause: Referenced cell error or access issue.
    - Resolution: Fix source; check permissions.
2. **#BOOLEAN EXPECTED**
    - Cause: Boolean column gets wrong type.
    - Resolution: Return 0/1; add "" for text.
3. **#CALCULATING**
    - Cause: Large sheet or complex refs.
    - Resolution: Wait; optimize ranges; archive rows.
4. **#CIRCULAR REFERENCE**
    - Cause: Self-reference loop.
    - Resolution: Break loop; test parts.
5. **#CONTACT EXPECTED**
    - Cause: Contact column gets non-contact.
    - Resolution: Return text/contact.
6. **#DATE EXPECTED**
    - Cause: Date column gets non-date.
    - Resolution: Use DATE/DATEONLY.
7. **#DIVIDE BY ZERO**
    - Cause: /0.
    - Resolution: IFERROR or check denominator.
8. **#IMBALANCED**
    - Cause: Mismatched parentheses.

- Resolution: Balance ().

9. **#INCORRECT ARGUMENT SET**
    - Cause: Mismatched ranges/args.
    - Resolution: Align sizes; check syntax.
10. **#INVALID COLUMN VALUE**
    - Cause: Type mismatch for column.
    - Resolution: Match types.
11. **#INVALID DATA TYPE**
    - Cause: Wrong type in function.
    - Resolution: Convert with VALUE.

1. **#INVALID OPERATION**
    - Cause: Incompatible types.
    - Resolution: Convert.
2. **#INVALID REF**
    - Cause: Deleted ref.
    - Resolution: Recreate in manager.
3. **#NO MATCH**
    - Cause: Lookup failure.
    - Resolution: IFERROR; check spelling/case.
4. **#NUMBER EXPECTED**
    - Cause: Number column gets non-number.
    - Resolution: Return number.
5. **#PARSEERROR**
    - Cause: Syntax error.
    - Resolution: Check commas/operators.
6. **#REF**
    - Cause: Invalid cell ref.
    - Resolution: Fix ref.
7. **#UNPARSEABLE**
    - Cause: Missing = or quotes.
    - Resolution: Verify structure.

Tips:

- Debug: Copy to notepad; test subsets.
- Flashing Errors: Refresh page.
- Wrong Refs: Use @row.
- Large Sheets: Split data.

Congratulations you're now ready to master Smartsheet formulas! Practice and build complexity gradually.

Chapter 6: Collaboration and Sharing

Collaboration is Smartsheet's strength. This chapter expands on permissions, methods, and tools.

Permissions Levels Detailed

- **Viewer**: Read-only, no edits.
- **Editor**: Edit cells/rows, add discussions.
- **Admin**: All above + manage sharing/automations.
- **Owner**: Full control, including delete.

How to Share

1. **Share Item**: Click Share > Add emails > Set level > Send.
2. **Workspaces**: Share entire folders for grouped access.
3. **Publishing**: For broad access, File > Publish > Generate link (read-only or edit). Options: Link-only, plan members, or shared users. Embed via iFrame.

Features for Teamwork

- **Comments/Attachments**: Right-click row > Comment or Attach file (up to 100MB). View in Activity Log.
- **Real-Time Edits**: Changes sync instantly; lock cells/rows to prevent edits.

- **@Mentions**: Type @name in comments to notify via email/app.
- **Proofing**: Upload files for review/approvals (premium).

Examples and Best Practices

- **Scenario**: Share a report with viewers for status updates, editors for inputs.
- **Tips**: Use "Edit by Anyone" cautiously for public links. Track changes in History.
- **Pitfalls**: Over-sharing sensitive data—use permissions wisely.

Pro Tip: Publish dashboards for stakeholder views without logins.

Chapter 7: Reports, Dashboards, and Visuals

Visualize data beyond sheets. For detailed creation guides, see the expanded sections below.

Reports: A Comprehensive Guide

Reports summarize data from multiple sources, enabling centralized views without duplicating data. They are row-based, support filtering, grouping, sorting, and summaries, but do not include sheet hierarchies or formulas (use sheet-level for those).

Step-by-Step Creation of a Report

1. **Start New Report**: From Home, click "Create" > "Report," or in the left sidebar under Reports > "+ New Report."
2. **Choose Report Type**:
    - **Row Report**: Standard for pulling row data (most common for beginners).
    - Name the report (e.g., "Overdue Tasks Report").

1. **Select Sources**:
    - Click "Add Source" > Choose sheets, folders, or workspaces.

- For multiple: Select a workspace to auto-include all sheets (dynamic for new additions).
- Tip: Start with one sheet for simplicity; add more as needed.

2. **Customize Columns**:
   - Select which columns to include from sources.
   - Reorder by dragging; add "Sheet Name" for context in multi-source reports.
3. **Add Filters**:
   - Click "Filters" > Add criteria (e.g., "Status = In Progress" or "Due Date < TODAY()").
   - Use AND/OR logic; up to 50 conditions.
   - Advanced: "Current User" for personalized views (e.g., my tasks only).

1. **Group Data**:
   - Click "Grouping" > Choose column (e.g., group by "Assignee").
   - Expandable groups; multi-level (up to 3).
2. **Add Summaries**:
   - Click "Summaries" > Add metrics (SUM, COUNT) for groups or overall.
   - Place at top/bottom; no custom formatting.
3. **Sort Data**:
   - Click "Sorting" > Add levels (e.g., by "Due Date" ascending).
   - Within groups if grouped.
4. **Save and View**:
   - Save; report opens in table view.
   - Edit source data directly (if Editor+ permissions).

1. **Share or Publish**: Share like sheets; publish for read-only links.

Report Features and Customization

- **Types**: Row reports (detail); no hierarchy from sources.
- **Source Selection**: Sheets/folders/workspaces; auto-include new sheets in workspaces.
- **Customization**:
    - Columns: Select/reorder; include Sheet Name for context.
    - Filters: AND/OR criteria; e.g., "Status = In Progress" OR "Priority = High".
    - Groups: By column (e.g., by Department); expandable.
    - Summaries: Metrics like SUM/COUNT in groups; no custom formatting.
    - Sorting: Multi-level, within groups.
- **Advanced Features**: Current User filters (personalized); edit source data directly (if permitted).
- **Sharing/Editing**: Viewer+ to see; Editor+ to modify; publish for read-only.

Examples and Use Cases for Reports

- **Basic**: "Overdue Tasks" report – Sources: One project sheet; Filter: Due < TODAY(); Sort by Priority descending.
- **Advanced**: Multi-sheet sales report – Sources: All regional sheets; Group by Region; Summarize SUM(Sales); Filter Year = 2025.
- **Use Cases**: Executive summaries, team metrics, audit trails.

Best Practices, Tips, and Pitfalls for Reports

- **Practices**: Build from key sheets; use for KPIs; refresh manually.

- **Tips**: Embed in dashboards; export to PDF/Excel; use for personalized views.
- **Pitfalls**: Blank if not shared to sources; large reports slow—filter aggressively.
- **Limitations**: No formulas in reports; 50,000 rows max display.
- **Troubleshooting**: No data? Check source sharing/permissions; filters too strict—remove one by one; #BLOCKED? Verify access.

Pro Tip: Build reports first, then widget them into dashboards.

Dashboards: A Comprehensive Guide

Dashboards visualize data with widgets, creating interactive overviews for teams or stakeholders. They pull from sheets/reports without storing data, updating dynamically.

Step-by-Step Creation of a Dashboard

1. **Start New Dashboard**: From Home, click "Create" > "Dashboard," or sidebar > "+ New Dashboard."
2. **Name and Location**: Enter name (e.g., "Project Overview"); save in workspace/folder.
3. **Add Widgets**: Click "+" in the toolbar or canvas > Choose type (detailed below).
    - Drag/resize on the canvas; arrange in grids.
4. **Configure Widgets**:
    - For each, select source (sheet/report) and customize (e.g., metric formula, chart type).

1. **Customize Layout**:
    - Themes: Colors, backgrounds (Settings > Theme).
    - Interactions: Click-to-open sources.

2. **Add Interactivity**: Enable drill-down (e.g., click metric to sheet).
3. **Save and Refresh**: Auto-saves; manual refresh for updates.
4. **Share or Publish**: Share button for collaborators; File > Publish for links/embeds.

Dashboard Widget Types and Details

Widgets are building blocks; up to 50 per dashboard.

- **Metric**: Display KPIs/formulas (e.g., =COUNTIF(Status:Status, "Done")).
- **Chart**: Bar/pie/line from sheet data; dynamic filters. In 2025, AI-powered chart creation builds and updates charts automatically.
- **Report**: Embed live reports (interactive if permitted).
- **Rich Text**: Instructions/links/images.
- **Image/Shortcut**: Visuals or quick links to sheets.
- **Title**: Headers for sections.

Customization and Features

- **Layout**: Drag/resize; group in sections.
- **Interactivity**: Drill-down to sources; auto-refresh every 10 minutes.
- **Publishing**: File > Publish > ON; options: Read-only, access controls (link, plan users).
- **Advanced**: iFrame embeds; default views for linked items.

Examples and Use Cases for Dashboards

- **Basic**: Team status – Widgets: Progress metric, overdue chart, rich text notes.

- **Advanced**: Executive – Embedded report, line chart trends, shortcut to details.
- **Use Cases**: Stakeholder portals, project tracking, KPI monitoring.

Best Practices, Tips, and Pitfalls for Dashboards

- **Practices**: Limit to 20 widgets for speed; prioritize key info.
- **Tips**: Use for mobile views; integrate with automations (update on change).
- **Pitfalls**: Overcrowding reduces usability; widgets blank? Check source sharing.
- **Limitations**: 50 widgets max; no advanced charting like heatmaps; no custom refresh.
- **Troubleshooting**: Blank widgets? Refresh sources/ permissions; slow load? Reduce widgets; #NO DATA? Verify formulas/filters.

Pro Tip: Publish for stakeholder portals without logins.

Chapter 8: Forms and Data Collection

Forms simplify input without sheet access. In 2025, forms have been updated for a modern, accessible experience, with smoother submission and enhanced usability.

Step-by-Step Creation

1. **From Sheet**: Forms > Create Form > Drag fields from columns.
2. **Customize**: Add logic (show fields based on answers), branding (logo/colors), captcha for spam.
3. **Share**: Get link/embed code. Submissions add as new rows.

Advanced Options

- **Field Types**: Match sheet columns, add hidden defaults.
- **Notifications**: Auto-email on submit.

Examples and Tips

- **Scenario**: Event RSVP form with name, email, attendance (dropdown).
- **Tips**: Use for surveys/polls. Track responses in sheet.
- **Pitfalls**: Forgetting logic can confuse users—test forms.

Pro Tip: Embed in websites for seamless collection.

Chapter 9: Automations and Alerts

Automate to save time that is beginner-friendly with no code. For a detailed guide, see the expanded section below.

Setup Basics

- **Create Workflow**: Automation > Create > Choose trigger (e.g., date reached, row changed).
- **Actions**: Alert someone, move/copy row, assign people, update cell.
- **Conditions**: Filter like "If Status = Done, approve request."

Common Examples

- Alert: Email on due date.
- Approval: Route for sign-off.
- Update: Auto-set status on checkbox.

Tips and Pitfalls

- **Scenario**: Remind assignee if task overdue.
- **Tips**: Start with alerts. Test workflows.
- **Pitfalls**: Over-automation causes spam—add conditions.

Pro Tip: Use for reminders to keep projects on track.

Automations: A Comprehensive Beginner-to-Advanced User Guide

Smartsheet automations streamline repetitive tasks by creating workflows that respond to changes in your sheets, such as sending alerts, requesting approvals, or moving rows. They're similar to conditional rules in other tools but integrated into Smartsheet's collaborative platform for efficiency and scalability. In 2025, automations include AI-powered predictive capabilities to anticipate delays and auto-assign resources.

This guide assumes you have a Smartsheet account (Pro, Business, or Enterprise plan) with at least Editor permissions on a sheet (Owner or Admin for full management). We'll start with basics and progress to advanced concepts, covering creation, revisions, and troubleshooting. By the end, you'll be able to build, modify, and debug automations confidently.

Introduction to Smartsheet Automations

Automations in Smartsheet replace manual processes with flexible workflows that trigger based on sheet changes or schedules. Key components include triggers (when to run), conditions (filters for specificity), and actions (what to do). Benefits include time savings, reduced errors, improved collaboration, and scalability for teams.

Common use cases:

- Send alerts for deadlines.
- Request updates or approvals.
- Move or copy rows between sheets.
- Lock/unlock rows for security.
- Assign tasks or record dates automatically.

Automations can be simple (one trigger-action) or complex (multi-path with conditions). Bridge (a premium add-on) extends to advanced integrations, but we'll focus on core automations first.

Automation Basics

How to Create an Automation

1. **Open the Automation Menu**: In the upper-left corner of your sheet, click Automation > Create workflow.
2. **Choose a Starting Point**:
    - From Template: Select Create from template for pre-built options (e.g., "Alert on deadline").
    - From Scratch: Select Create from scratch for custom setups.
3. **Set the Trigger**:
    - Choose when the workflow runs, e.g., "When a row is added or changed" or "On a schedule" (daily, weekly, etc.).
4. **Add Conditions (Optional)**: Filter rows, e.g., only if "Status" is "Complete".
5. **Define Actions**: Specify what happens, e.g., "Send an alert" or "Request approval".
6. **Configure Details**: Customize recipients, messages, or fields.
7. **Save and Activate**: Name the workflow, save, and toggle to active.

Example: Basic alert workflow.

- Trigger: When "Status" changes to "Complete".
- Condition: None.
- Action: Alert team via email.

To apply to multiple sheets, create in a template or duplicate.

Workflow Components

- **Triggers**: Events like row changes, date reached, or schedule. Details: Cells with formulas/links don't trigger sheet-modifying actions; use schedules as workaround.

- **Conditions**: Up to 20 per block, logical filters (AND/OR). Paths branch for different outcomes.
- **Actions**: Alerts, approvals, row moves, locks, assignments. Up to 30 actions per workflow, 100 blocks total.
- **Paths**: Left-to-right evaluation; each must end with an action.

Tips for Beginners

- Start with templates to learn structure.
- Use the workflow builder's drag-and-drop interface.
- Test in a sandbox sheet.
- Name workflows clearly (e.g., "Deadline Alert - Project X").
- Limits: 150 workflows per sheet; run hourly for time-based.
- Permissions: Editors can create; Admins manage all.

Detailed Workflow Creation
Step-by-Step: Creating from Template

1. Click Automation > Create from template.
2. Browse categories (e.g., "Alerts & Reminders").
3. Select a template, review details/tips.
4. Customize: Edit trigger, add conditions, modify action.
5. Save and activate.

Example: "Alert on upcoming deadline" template.

- Trigger: Date in "Due Date" column.
- Condition: Due Date is in the next 3 days.
- Action: Alert assigned person.

Step-by-Step: Creating from Scratch

1. Click Automation > Create from scratch.
2. Add Trigger Block: Select type (change, schedule).
3. Add Condition Block: Click + , set paths (e.g., if "Priority = High").
4. Add Action Block: Choose action, configure (e.g., email message, recipients).
5. Connect Blocks: Drag to form flowchart.
6. Test: Save, make a sheet change to trigger.

Advanced Example: Approval Workflow.

- Trigger: Row added.
- Condition: If "Amount > 1000".
- Path 1 (True): Request approval from manager.
- Path 2 (False): Auto-approve and assign task.
- Action: Update cell to "Approved" on approval.

Triggers in Depth

- **Change-Based**: When rows added/changed (specific columns).
- **Date-Based**: When a date is reached (e.g., start/end).
- **Schedule**: Recurring (hourly to annually).
- Parameters: Run as user or system; time offsets (e.g., 1 hour before).

Example: Schedule trigger for weekly report – run every Monday at 9 AM.

Conditions in Depth

- Add via + icon; up to 20 statements.
- Operators: Equals, Greater Than, Contains, etc.
- Logic: AND (all true), OR (any true).

- Paths: Multiple for branching (e.g., High/Medium/Low priority).

Example: Condition – "If Status = Complete AND Assignee = John".

Actions in Depth

- **Alert/Notification**: Email/Slack/in-app; customize message with placeholders (e.g., {{Row ID}}).
- **Request Update/Approval**: Send form-like request; track responses.
- **Move/Copy Row**: To another sheet; map columns.
- **Lock/Unlock Row**: Prevent edits.
- **Assign People**: Update contact column.
- **Record Date**: Stamp current date.
- **Change Cell**: Set value.

Example: Move row action – when "Status = Archive", move to archive sheet.

Revisions and Management

Editing an Existing Automation

1. Click Automation > Manage workflows.
2. Select the workflow, click Edit.
3. Modify: Add/remove blocks, adjust conditions, change actions.
4. Save changes; test by triggering.

Example: Revise alert to include condition – edit to add "If Priority = High".

Duplicating a Workflow

1. In Manage workflows, select and click Duplicate.

2. Rename and modify as needed (e.g., change recipients).
3. Activate the copy; deactivate original if obsolete.

Tip: Duplicate for variations (e.g., team-specific alerts).

Deactivating/Deleting

- Toggle off in Manage to pause.
- Delete if unused, but confirm – irreversible.

Versioning and Revisions Best Practices

- No built-in versioning; duplicate before major changes.
- Track changes manually in comments or a log sheet.
- Review periodically: In Manage, check run history for issues.

Advanced: Use Bridge for custom revisions (e.g., API-based edits).

Advanced Automations

Multi-Path Workflows

- Branch conditions for different actions (e.g., approve if < $500, escalate if >).
- Up to multiple paths; evaluate left-to-right.

Integrations with Bridge

- Premium add-on for advanced: API calls, JavaScript, external tools (e.g., Google, ServiceNow).
- Build: Triggers, branching, modules (HTTP, API).
- Example: Trigger on sheet change, integrate with time-tracking system.

Time-Based and Recurrence

- Schedule: Hourly to yearly; offsets for precision.
- Workaround for formula cells: Use recurrence instead of change triggers.

Permissions in Depth

- Creators: Editor+.
- Runners: As user (personal) or system (impersonal).
- Shared: Workflow follows sheet sharing.

Best Practices

- Keep simple: Start with 1-2 conditions.
- Test thoroughly: Use test rows, check emails.
- Optimize: Combine related workflows; deactivate unused.
- Security: Avoid sensitive data in messages.
- Scale: Use templates for consistency across sheets.
- Monitor: Check run history in Manage for failures.

Troubleshooting Guide

Common issues, causes, solutions:

1. **Workflow Not Triggering**
    - Cause: Trigger mismatch (e.g., formula cells don't trigger modifications).
    - Solution: Use schedule/recurrence; verify permissions (Editor+ needed).
2. **Delayed Execution**
    - Cause: Large sheets or backend load.
    - Solution: Wait a few minutes; set triggers 1 hour early.

3. **#BLOCKED or Permission Errors**
    - Cause: Insufficient sheet access for runner/recipients.
    - Solution: Share sheet with users; use system-run for broad access.
4. **Actions Not Performing (e.g., No Email)**
    - Cause: Conditions not met; email blocked.
    - Solution: Test conditions; check spam; verify placeholders.
5. **Invalid Workflow Structure**
    - Cause: Paths without actions; >100 blocks.
    - Solution: Add actions to ends; simplify.
6. **Approval/Update Failures**
    - Cause: Duplicated workflows triggering old approvals.
    - Solution: Modify requests in duplicates.

1. **Cross-Sheet Issues (e.g., Move Row Fails)**
    - Cause: Target sheet permissions; column mismatch.
    - Solution: Map columns; ensure Admin access.
2. **Attachment Links Expire**
    - Cause: 14-day limit.
    - Solution: Notify recipients to access promptly.
3. **General Errors (#UNPARSEABLE-like)**
    - Cause: Syntax in conditions/placeholders.
    - Solution: Double-check logic; use builder previews.

Tips:

- Run History: In Manage, view logs for failures.
- Debug: Deactivate, test isolated parts.

You've now got the tools to master Smartsheet automations! Practice and iterate.

Chapter 10: Advanced Basics – Integrations and Mobile

Extend Smartsheet's reach.

Integrations Details

- **Built-In**: Google Workspace (import sheets), Microsoft (Outlook calendar sync), Slack (notifications).
- **Setup**: Marketplace > Add app > Authorize.
- **Examples**: Zapier for custom (e.g., new form submit > create Trello card).

Mobile App Overview

- **Features**: Edit sheets, view dashboards, scan barcodes, offline mode (syncs later).
- **Differences**: Touch-optimized, but no advanced editing like formulas.

Tips

- **Scenario**: Mobile for field data entry.
- **Pitfalls**: Battery drain on large sheets—use web for heavy work.

Pro Tip: Integrate with Teams for chat-based updates.

Chapter 11: Tips, Tricks, and Common Pitfalls for Beginners

Compile best practices for success.

Top Tips

- **Organization**: Use workspaces for projects, color-code rows.
- **Efficiency**: Shortcuts like Ctrl+Z undo, filters for views.
- **Learning**: Complete Level 1 track (1-2 hours).

- **Backup**: Export weekly to Excel.
- **Community**: Forum for questions.

Common Pitfalls

- Ignoring hierarchy—flattens complex data.
- Formula errors—debug with IFERROR.
- Sharing mishaps—review permissions.

Advanced Tricks

- Use Bridge for custom integrations.
- Dynamic views for filtered sharing.

Final Note: Practice daily and start a personal sheet for groceries or habits. Happy Smartsheeting!

Intermediate Level

Welcome to this expanded, in-depth intermediate guide for Smartsheet! Building on foundational concepts, we go much deeper into each chapter with exhaustive details, including advanced sub-features, step-by-step processes with variations, real-world examples, integration ideas, troubleshooting, limitations, best practices, and common pitfalls. This is tailored for users comfortable with basics but wanting to master scalable workflows. Let's level up your Smartsheet expertise!

Chapter 1: Introduction to Intermediate Workflows

Intermediate workflows in Smartsheet transform static data management into dynamic, automated systems that support team collaboration and decision-making. At this level, you'll integrate features like forms for input, automations for processing, reports for analysis, and dashboards for visualization, creating end-to-end processes that reduce manual effort and minimize errors.

Key Concepts and Objectives

- **Workflow Components**: Data collection (forms), monitoring (tracking/activity logs), customization (sorting/filtering/formatting), notification (alerts/actions), automation (multi-step rules), aggregation (linking/reports), visualization (dashboards), and distribution (sharing/publishing).
- **Learning Goals**: Design workflows that handle complex scenarios, such as conditional routing or cross-sheet data syncing; optimize for performance in large datasets; ensure security and auditability.
- **Why Deeper Now?**: Beginners focus on single sheets; intermediates build interconnected systems. For example, a workflow might start with a form submission, trigger an

automation to assign tasks, update a report for managers, and display KPIs on a dashboard.

Building a Sample Intermediate Workflow

1. **Plan the Flow**: Identify inputs (e.g., new project requests via forms), processes (e.g., auto-approve low-risk items), outputs (e.g., dashboard metrics).
2. **Scale Considerations**: Handle up to 20,000 rows per sheet; use workspaces for organization (up to unlimited in paid plans).
3. **Integration Overview**: Connect with external tools like Zapier for non-native actions (e.g., post to Slack on approval).

Best Practices and Pitfalls

- **Practices**: Start with a workflow map (use a Smartsheet template for this); test in a sandbox workspace.
- **Pitfalls**: Overcomplicating early- Try and begin with 2-3 features per workflow; ignoring user permissions can lead to data exposure.
- **Troubleshooting**: If workflows fail, check activity logs for errors.
- **Limitations**: Free plans limit automations (e.g., 2 per sheet); Enterprise offers advanced governance like audit trails.

Pro Tip: Enroll in Smartsheet University's Level 2 track (2-4 hours) for interactive modules on these workflows.

Chapter 2: Collecting Data Using Forms

Forms elevate data entry by enabling structured, user-friendly collection from internal teams or external stakeholders, feeding directly into sheets. At intermediate level, emphasize logic, branding, and integrations for robust intake processes.

Detailed Setup and Customization

- **Creation Steps**:
  - Open a sheet > Forms > Create Form (or Manage Forms for existing).
  - Auto-generated fields from sheet columns; drag to reorder or add headers/descriptions.
  - Customize: Set required fields, add help text, enable CAPTCHA for public forms.
- **Advanced Logic and Validation**:
  - Conditional Logic: Show/hide fields based on responses (e.g., if "Department = HR," show "Employee ID" field). Supports up to 100 rules; use AND/OR for complex branching.
  - Validation: Email/phone formats, unique values, character limits.
  - Hidden Fields: Pre-fill with defaults (e.g., submission timestamp via system column) or URL parameters.
- **Branding and User Experience**:
  - Add logos, colors, custom headers/footers; embed forms in websites via iFrame.
  - Confirmation: Custom messages or redirects post-submission.
- **Sharing and Security**:
  - Generate links; restrict to domain emails.
  - Permissions: Submitters don't need Smartsheet access; responses append as new rows.

Integrations and Advanced Features

- **With Automations**: Trigger workflows on submission (e.g., notify approver).
- **With External Tools**: Use Webhooks or Zapier to sync to Google Forms alternatives or CRM systems.
- **Pre-Fills**: Via URL queries for personalized forms (e.g., pre-populate user name from email link).

Examples and Use Cases

- **Scenario**: IT Support Ticket System—Fields: Issue Type (dropdown), Description (text), Urgency (radio). Logic: If "Hardware," show "Device Model." Submissions auto-assign via automation.
- **Advanced Example**: Event Registration—Multi-select for sessions; validate attendee count against limits using formulas in the backend sheet.

Tips, Troubleshooting, and Pitfalls

- **Tips**: Test forms in incognito mode; use mobile preview for responsiveness.
- **Troubleshooting**: If submissions don't appear, check sheet permissions or spam filters for notifications.
- **Pitfalls**: Too many logic rules slow form loading; forgetting to save changes loses customizations.
- **Limitations**: 100 fields max; no file uploads in free plans (pro unlocks attachments).

Pro Tip: Analyze submission trends with reports on form data for process improvements.

Chapter 3: Tracking and Viewing Activity in Your Sheet

Tracking ensures transparency and accountability, allowing you to audit changes, resolve disputes, and maintain data integrity. Intermediate users leverage this for compliance and performance monitoring.

Core Features and Access

- **Highlight Changes**:
    - Toolbar > Highlight Changes > Toggle ON.
    - Options: Since last view, specific time frames (1-90 days), colors for edits/comments/attachments.
    - Applies to cells, rows, or entire sheet; resets on refresh.
- **Cell History**:
    - Right-click cell > View Cell History.
    - Shows chronological changes: Old/new values, user, timestamp; restore previous if needed.
- **Activity Log**:
    - File > View Activity Log.
    - Tracks: Edits, views, shares, deletions, automations; filters by user/action/date.
    - Export to CSV; retention: 90 days (Enterprise: customizable).
- **System Columns for Tracking**: Add Modified Date/By, Created Date/By for row-level audits.

Advanced Usage and Integrations

- **Notifications Tie-In**: Set alerts for specific changes (e.g., high-value cell edits).
- **With Reports**: Pull activity data into reports for aggregated audits (though logs aren't directly reportable).

- **Conversations Panel**: View all comments/attachments in one place; filter by row.

Examples and Scenarios

- **Use Case**: Project Audit- Highlight changes since last review to spot unauthorized edits; use log to trace who modified budget cells.
- **Advanced**: Compliance Workflow- Export logs monthly for regulatory reviews; combine with conditional formatting to flag anomalies.

Tips, Troubleshooting, and Pitfalls

- **Tips**: Use in conjunction with locked rows to prevent unwanted changes while tracking.
- **Troubleshooting**: If log is empty, check user permissions (Admin+ required); browser cache can hide highlights.
- **Pitfalls**: Logs don't capture report views; overlooking retention period loses historical data.
- **Limitations**: No real-time log streaming; max 10,000 entries visible at once.

Pro Tip: Automate log exports via Bridge (premium add-on) for long-term archiving.

Chapter 4: Custom Sorting and Filtering Views

Sorting and filtering create personalized, dynamic views for efficient data navigation, essential for intermediate analysis in large sheets.

Sorting: In-Depth Mechanics

- **Steps**:

  - Right-click column header > Sort Rows.
  - Choose criteria: Ascending/descending, multi-column (up to 3 levels, e.g., Priority then Due Date).
  - Scope: All rows or selected; preserves hierarchy (parents/children stay grouped).
- **Special Handling**: Symbols (e.g., checkboxes: unchecked first); dates (chronological); numbers (numeric order).
- **Interactions**: Sorting is permanent after save; can't sort while filtered; locked rows immovable by non-Admins.

Filtering: Advanced Criteria

- **Creation**:
  - Filter > New Filter > Name it (for saving/sharing).
  - Add conditions: Equals, contains, is blank, etc.; AND/OR logic; row-based (e.g., has attachments, on critical path requires dependencies enabled).
- **Advanced Options**: Current User (e.g., show my tasks); dependencies (predecessors/successors); up to 50 conditions.
- **Saving/Sharing**: Named filters shareable (Business+); apply to views like Gantt/Card.

Examples and Integrations

- **Scenario**: Sales Pipeline- Filter "Stage = Negotiation" AND "Value > $10k"; sort by Close Date ascending.
- **Advanced**: Personal Dashboard View- Filter "Assignee = Current User" OR "Watcher = Current User"; integrate with reports for cross-sheet filtering.

Tips, Troubleshooting, and Pitfalls

- **Tips**: Use parentheses in complex criteria for grouping; convert data types (e.g., text to number via formula) for better filtering.
- **Troubleshooting**: Filters not applying? Check column types; refresh sheet.
- **Pitfalls**: Sorting flattens unsaved changes; shared filters override personal ones if not managed.
- **Limitations**: No regex in criteria; 400 columns max impacts performance.

Pro Tip: Combine with conditional formatting for visually filtered views.

Chapter 5: Conditional Formatting

Conditional formatting applies visual rules to highlight trends, risks, or statuses, turning data into actionable insights.

Rule Creation and Management

- **Steps**:
    - Format > Conditional Formatting > Add Rule.
    - Set criteria: Cell value (e.g., >50), formula (e.g., =IF([Due Date]@row < TODAY() - 7, TRUE)).
    - Apply format: Background/color, bold/italic, strike-through; to entire row or column.
- **Prioritization**: Drag rules to reorder; higher rules override lower if conflicting.
- **Formula Advanced**: Use @row, CHILDREN(), or cross-sheet refs; test with IF/AND/OR.

Examples and Use Cases

- **Basic**: Red row if "Status = Delayed".
- **Advanced**: Gradient based on % Complete (e.g., green

>80%, yellow 50-80%, red <50% via multiple rules); flag overdue with =TODAY() - [Date]@row > 0.

Integrations and Tips

- **With Views**: Enhances Gantt (color bars) or Card (label colors).
- **Tips**: Use for heat maps (e.g., risk matrix); duplicate rules for variations.
- **Troubleshooting**: Rules not firing? Check formula syntax; disable/re-enable.
- **Pitfalls**: Over 100 rules slow sheets; formulas recalculate on every change.
- **Limitations**: No custom icons beyond basics; doesn't export to PDF perfectly.

Pro Tip: Pair with automations to update cells that trigger formatting.

Chapter 6: Alerts and Actions

Alerts and actions form the foundation of proactive workflows, notifying users or requesting inputs based on triggers.

Types and Detailed Setup

- **Alerts/Reminders**: Notify on changes (e.g., row added) or dates (e.g., 3 days before due).
- **Update Requests**: Prompt for data (e.g., "Update status").
- **Approvals**: Route decisions (e.g., approve/reject with comments).
- **Steps**:
    - Automation > Create Workflow > Select trigger (change/date/form).
    - Add conditions (e.g., if Priority = High).

    - Choose action; personalize message with placeholders ({{[Column]@row}}).
- **Advanced**: Schedule reminders (recurring); include attachments/links.

Examples and Scenarios

- **Use Case**: Overdue Alert- Trigger: Date reached, Condition: Status != Done, Action: Email assignee.
- **Advanced**: Approval Chain- If amount > $5k, request manager approval; branch on response.

Tips, Troubleshooting, and Pitfalls

- **Tips**: Use for escalation (e.g., if no response in 24h, alert supervisor).
- **Troubleshooting**: No email? Check spam/do-not-disturb settings.
- **Pitfalls**: Vague messages confuse users; too many alerts lead to fatigue.
- **Limitations**: 100 workflows per sheet; no custom branding in emails.

Pro Tip: Transition to full automations (see Chapter 7) for multi-action sequences.

Chapter 7: Automate Your Workflows

Full automations orchestrate complex processes, automating repetitive tasks across sheets and tools.

Workflow Builder Deep Dive

- **Triggers**: Row changes, dates reached, form submissions, schedules (e.g., daily at 9AM).

- **Actions**: Move/copy rows, assign contacts, lock/unlock, update cells, send alerts.
- **Conditions/Branches**: If/else paths (e.g., if Approved, move to "Done" sheet; else, request revisions).
- **Steps**:
    - Automation > Create > Build visually (drag blocks).
    - Test run on sample data.
- **Advanced**: Loops (careful to avoid infinite); integrations (e.g., Jira sync via Bridge).

Examples and Integrations

- **Scenario**: Onboarding Workflow- Form submit > Auto-assign HR > Approval > Copy to employee sheet > Alert manager.
- **Advanced**: Inventory Auto-Reorder—If stock < threshold, create purchase row in another sheet.

Tips, Troubleshooting, and Pitfalls

- **Tips**: Use error handling (e.g., notify on failure); version workflows.
- **Troubleshooting**: Debug via run history; check quotas.
- **Pitfalls**: Self-triggers cause loops; untested automations corrupt data.
- **Limitations**: 250 actions per workflow; premium for advanced triggers.

Pro Tip: Monitor usage in Account Admin for optimization.

Chapter 8: Using Cell Linking and Reporting

Cell linking and reporting connect and summarize data, enabling centralized views without duplication. In 2025, column links allow additional inbound and outbound links for better cross-sheet syncing.

Cell Linking Details

- **Steps**: Right-click > Link from Cell in Another Sheet > Select source range.
- **Advanced**: One-way sync (source updates target); use for rollups (e.g., sum from child sheets).
- **Limitations**: 100,000 inbound links per sheet; breaks if source deleted.

Reporting: Exhaustive Guide

For a complete guide to reports, see Beginner Level Chapter 7. At intermediate level, focus on multi-source aggregation and integration with dashboards.

- **Advanced Examples**: Overdue Tasks Report—Sources: All project sheets; Filter: Due < TODAY(); Group by Assignee; Summarize: COUNT per group.
- **Tips**: Link cells in a master sheet, then report on it for hybrid aggregation.

Pro Tip: Use for KPIs; refresh manually for latest data.

Chapter 9: Dashboards for Visualization

Dashboards provide at-a-glance overviews with widgets, ideal for executive summaries. For a complete guide, see Beginner Level Chapter 7. At intermediate level, emphasize customization and interactivity.

Setup and Widget Deep Dive

- **Widget Types**: Metric for KPIs, Chart for graphs (AI-powered in 2025 for auto-build), Report for embeds, Rich

Text for notes.

- **Customization**: Drag/resize widgets, add images/links. Share like sheets.
- **Use Cases**: Dashboard with report widget for team metrics, chart for progress.
- **Tips**: Use for executive summaries. Refresh manually if data changes.
- **Pitfalls**: Too many widgets slow loading so try to prioritize key info.

Pro Tip: Build reports first, then widget them into dashboards.

Chapter 10: Sharing Your Insights

Sharing distributes workflows securely, from individual items to bundled apps.

Methods and Permissions

- **Item Sharing**: Share button > Add users/groups > Set level (Viewer/Editor/Admin/Owner).
- **Workspaces**: Group share for bulk access.
- **Publishing**: Read-only links (as in dashboards); edit-by-anyone for crowdsourcing.
- **Advanced**: Dynamic Views (filtered shares); WorkApps (bundle sheets/reports/dashboards into apps with roles).

Security and Best Practices

- **Groups**: Create for teams (Admin > User Management).
- **Licensed vs Unlicensed**: Unlicensed can view/edit if shared.
- **Examples**: Share report with Viewers for status; publish dashboard publicly.

Tips, Troubleshooting, and Pitfalls

- **Tips**: Use audit logs to track shares; revoke via Manage Sharing.
- **Troubleshooting**: Access denied? Check inheritance from workspaces.
- **Pitfalls**: Default to over-sharing so start restrictive.
- **Limitations**: Free plans limit collaborators (10 per item).

Pro Tip: Use WorkApps for client portals with branded interfaces.

Chapter 11: Tips, Tricks, and Pitfalls for Intermediate Users

Compile advanced strategies to maximize efficiency.

Efficiency Tricks

- **Shortcuts**: Ctrl+Shift+F (filter), Alt+Shift+> (indent row).
- **Optimization**: Index columns for faster formulas; archive old data to separate sheets.
- **Learning Resources**: Level 2 modules (1-2 hours each).
- **Custom Views**: Save filter/sort combos as personal defaults.

Common Pitfalls and Fixes

- **Data Loss**: Always backup via export; avoid deleting sources mid-workflow.
- **Performance**: Split large sheets; limit cross-sheet refs (<10,000).
- **Security**: Review permissions quarterly; use SSO in Enterprise.
- **Integration Issues**: Test Zapier zaps; monitor API limits if using.

Next Steps

- Advance to Level 3: Formulas, dependencies, Bridge for

custom code.
- Experiment: Build a full CRM workflow to apply all chapters.

This deep dive equips you for pro-level Smartsheet use! Practice these in a test workspace.

Advanced Level

Welcome to this comprehensive, detailed advanced guide for Smartsheet! As an experienced user transitioning from intermediate skills, this guide delves into enterprise-level features, complex integrations, and cutting-edge capabilities. We'll cover sophisticated tools to build scalable solutions, optimize performance, and leverage AI-driven innovations. Structured as a "book" with chapters, this draws from Smartsheet University Level 3 training, premium features, and API docs. Expect in-depth explanations, examples, code snippets (where applicable), use cases, best practices, pitfalls, and troubleshooting.

Chapter 1: Introduction to Advanced Smartsheet

Advanced Smartsheet usage focuses on scaling work management for enterprises: automating at scale, integrating disparate systems, deriving AI-powered insights, and ensuring governance. Level 3 (Solutions) in Smartsheet University emphasizes building complete solutions with advanced formulas, dependencies, and tools like Control Center.

Key Advanced Concepts

- **Enterprise Shift**: Move from single-sheet workflows to multi-sheet ecosystems with cross-references, blueprints, and API calls.
- **2025 Updates Overview**: AI for chart creation, enhanced

column links, smoother scrolling and responsive editing in table views, simplified dependency management, and predictive automation.

- **Prerequisites**: Mastery of Level 2 (e.g., alerts, cell linking, dashboards); access to Business/Enterprise plans for premium features like Bridge, DataMesh.

Getting Started with Advanced Tools

1. **Upgrade Path**: Switch to Enterprise for unlimited automations, advanced security (e.g., customer-managed keys), and AI features.
2. **Learning Resources**: Enroll in Smartsheet University's Advanced track (self-paced or instructor-led); pursue certifications like Control Center Lead.
3. **Sandbox Setup**: Create a dedicated workspace for testing advanced setups to avoid disrupting production.

Use Cases for Advanced Users

- Managing global teams: Use Control Center for standardized project blueprints.
- Data-driven decisions: Leverage AI analytics for predictive insights.

Best Practices and Pitfalls

- **Practices**: Map workflows end-to-end before implementation; use version history for audits.
- **Pitfalls**: Over-relying on complex formulas without optimization can slow sheets (limit to <10,000 cross-refs).
- **Troubleshooting**: If features are locked, check plan level in Account > Plan & Billing.

Pro Tip: Join the Smartsheet Community for peer-shared advanced templates.

Chapter 2: Advanced Formulas and Cross-Sheet References

Advanced formulas enable dynamic calculations across sheets, with functions for aggregation, logic, and error handling. 2025 introduces enhanced cross-sheet references with simplified management and additional column links.

Formula Syntax and Advanced Functions

- **Cross-Sheet Ranges**: Use {Range Name} for references (e.g., =SUM({Budget Sheet Range1})).
- **Key Functions**:
  - JOIN/COLLECT: =JOIN(COLLECT({Other Sheet Names}, {Other Sheet IDs}, ID@row), ", ") – Collects matching values.
  - INDEX/MATCH: =INDEX({Remote Range}, MATCH([Primary]@row, {Remote Primary}, 0)) – Faster than VLOOKUP.
  - CHILDREN/ANCESTORS: =SUM(CHILDREN()) for hierarchy rollups; ANCESTORS for path tracing.
  - Error Handling: =IFERROR(formula, "Error") or =IF(ISERROR(formula), "Custom Msg").

Column Links (2025 Feature)

- **Setup**: Right-click column > Link Column > Select source sheet/column; filters sync data dynamically.
- **Advantages**: No duplication; auto-updates; delete non-matching records.
- **Example**: Link "Project Status" column from master to detail sheets for real-time rollups.

Examples and Use Cases

- **Scenario**: Portfolio Metrics – =COUNTIFS({All Projects Status}, "At Risk", {All Projects Budget}, >100000) counts high-risk projects.
- **Advanced**: Nested IF with OR/AND: =IF(AND([Due Date]@row < TODAY(), OR([Status]@row = "In Progress", [Status]@row = "To Do")), "Overdue", "On Track").

Best Practices, Pitfalls, Troubleshooting

- **Practices**: Name ranges for readability; use helper columns for complex logic.
- **Pitfalls**: Circular refs (#CIRCULAR) – break with IF checks; performance dips over 100k cells – split sheets.
- **Troubleshooting**: #BLOCKED? Check sharing; use Formula Error Checker (fx icon > Debug).

Pro Tip: Export formulas to Excel for validation.

Chapter 3: Dependencies, Gantt, and Resource Management

Dependencies automate scheduling; advanced use includes resource allocation and critical path analysis. In 2025, dependency management is simplified for easier setup.

Enabling and Managing Dependencies

- **Setup**: Sheet Settings > Project Settings > Enable Dependencies.
- **Types**: FS (Finish-Start), SS, FF, SF; add lag/lead (e.g., FS+2d).
- **Critical Path**: Highlight via Gantt view; formula: =IF([On Critical Path]@row = 1, "Critical", "").

Resource Management (Premium)

- **Allocation**: Add Resource columns; view overload in Resource Views.
- **2025 Updates**: Enhanced scenario planning to compare "what-if" schedules and spot risks.

Examples and Use Cases

- **Scenario**: Multi-Project Timeline – Set predecessors; use Gantt for visuals.
- **Advanced**: Overload Formula: =IF([Allocated %]@row > 100, "Overloaded", "OK").

Best Practices, Pitfalls

- **Practices**: Use baselines for variance tracking; integrate with calendars.
- **Pitfalls**: Ignoring weekends – adjust working days in settings.
- **Troubleshooting**: Dates not updating? Check column types (Date).

Pro Tip: Use Card View for Kanban with dependencies.

Chapter 4: Advanced Automation and Workflows

Build multi-branch automations with conditions, approvals, and integrations. In 2025, AI-powered automation predicts delays and auto-assigns resources.

Workflow Builder Deep Dive

- **Triggers/Actions**: Schedules (daily), webhooks; actions like Jira sync via Bridge.
- **Branches**: If/Else for paths (e.g., If Budget > $10k, Require Approval).

Examples

- **Complex**: On form submit, if High Priority, assign VIP, else standard; notify via Slack.

Best Practices

- **Practices**: Use placeholders {{[Column]@row}}; test with duplicates.
- **Pitfalls**: Quota limits (Enterprise unlimited); loops – add conditions.
- **Troubleshooting**: View Run History; errors? Check logs.

Chapter 5: Control Center and Blueprints

Control Center scales solutions with blueprints for standardized projects.

Building Blueprints

- **Steps**: Control Center > New Blueprint > Add templates, automations.
- **Features**: Auto-provision projects, update rules.

Management and Certifications

- **Program Lead**: Manage portfolios.
- **Certifications**: Lead/Builder – verify skills in scaling.

Examples

- **Use Case**: Marketing Campaigns – Blueprint auto-creates sheets, assigns teams.

Best Practices

- **Practices**: Use metrics for portfolio health.
- **Pitfalls**: Template mismatches – version control.
- **Troubleshooting**: Access denied? Check licensing.

Pro Tip: Integrate with Data Shuttle for data imports.

Chapter 6: Data Connectivity: DataMesh, DataShuttle, Bridge

Connect external data seamlessly.

DataMesh

- **Description**: Sync lookup data across sheets; premium.
- **Setup**: Create config > Map fields; auto-updates.

DataShuttle

- **Description**: Import/export to/from external systems (e.g., SQL, CSV).
- **Integrations Panel (2025)**: Manage in table view.

Bridge

- **Description**: Custom workflows with JavaScript modules.
- **Example**: API calls to external services.

Use Cases

- **Advanced**: Sync CRM data to Smartsheet for reporting.

Best Practices

- **Practices**: Schedule runs; monitor logs.
- **Pitfalls**: Data mismatches – validate mappings.
- **Troubleshooting**: Errors? Check API keys.

Pro Tip: Use with AI for auto-insights.

Chapter 7: Advanced Reporting and Analytics

Aggregate multi-sheet data with summaries, groups. For basics, see Beginner Level Chapter 7.

Report Builder

- **Advanced**: Group by multiple levels; summaries (AVG, MAX); current user filters.

AI Analytics (2025)

- **Features**: Auto-summarize, generate charts.

Examples

- **Portfolio Report**: Sources: All projects; Group: Department; Summarize: SUM(Budget).

Best Practices

- **Practices**: Embed in dashboards; export PDF.
- **Pitfalls**: Row limits (50k) – filter aggressively.
- **Troubleshooting**: No data? Share sources.

Pro Tip: Use for burndown charts in analytics.

Chapter 8: Dashboards and Visualization (Advanced)

Create interactive overviews with widgets. For basics, see Beginner Level Chapter 7.

Advanced Widgets

- **Timeline View (2025)**: Map phases/milestones.
- **AI Charts**: Generate via natural language.

File Library (2025)

- **Description**: Centralize files with approvals.

Examples

- **Exec Dashboard**: Metrics, charts, embedded reports.

Best Practices

- **Practices**: Use interactions (click-to-sheet).
- **Pitfalls**: Overload (limit 50 widgets).
- **Troubleshooting**: Blank? Refresh sources.

Pro Tip: Publish for external stakeholders.

Chapter 9: API and Developer Integrations

Build custom apps with Smartsheet API. In 2025, API updates include new event types and webhook domain changes for better security.developers.

Advanced Topics

- **Cell Formatting**: Set via API (e.g., JSON: {"format": "bold"}).
- **Complex Columns**: Handle contacts, hyperlinks; compatibility checks.
- **OAuth**: Implement for secure auth; scopes like READ_SHEETS.
- **Scaling**: Pagination for large data; rate limits (300/min).

Code Snippet Example (Python)

```
import smartsheet
smartsheet_client = smartsheet.Smartsheet('YOUR_ACCESS_TOKEN')
sheet = smartsheet_client.Sheets.get_sheet(SHEET_ID)
```

Update cell

```
row_update = smartsheet.models.Row()
```

```
cell = smartsheet.models.Cell({'column_id': COLUMN_ID,
'value': 'New Value'})
row_update.cells.append(cell)
smartsheet_client.Sheets.update_rows(SHEET_ID,
[row_update])
```

Use Cases

- **Custom Integration**: Sync with CRM via API.

Best Practices

- **Practices**: Use webhooks for real-time.
- **Pitfalls**: Token expiry – refresh OAuth.
- **Troubleshooting**: 429 errors? Throttle requests.

Pro Tip: Explore SDKs (Java, .NET).

Chapter 10: Security, Governance, and Compliance

Enterprise controls for data protection.

Features

- **Encryption Keys**: Customer-managed via AWS KMS; rotate/revoke.
- **Data Egress Policy**: Block exports; notify on attempts.
- **Regions**: Select storage (e.g., EU for GDPR).
- **Activity Log**: Track changes; export for audits.

Examples

- **Compliance**: Retain data per policy; use DocuSign for e-signatures.

Best Practices

- **Practices**: Central admin for users; SSO integration.
- **Pitfalls**: Weak permissions – audit quarterly.
- **Troubleshooting**: Access logs? Filter by user.

Pro Tip: Enable 2FA; use groups for bulk access.

Chapter 11: New Features in 2025

Smartsheet's 2025 releases enhance AI, UI, and scalability.

AI Enhancements

- AI-powered chart creation in dashboards builds and updates charts automatically.
- Predictive automation to anticipate task delays and risks.
- Enhanced AI agents in integrations for smarter workflows.

UI and Data

- Redesigned table views with smoother scrolling and responsive editing.
- Modern forms for better accessibility and submission experience.
- Simplified dependency management and cross-sheet references with additional column links.

Data Shuttle

- Improved integrations panel for managing connections in table view.

Pro Tip: Check Smartsheet release notes for the latest rollout details.

Premium Add-ons to Smartsheet
Data Shuttle Overview

Welcome to this comprehensive guide on Data Shuttle, a premium add-on for Smartsheet designed to automate data movement between Smartsheet and external systems. Whether you're centralizing data from ERPs, CRMs, databases, or simple files, Data Shuttle streamlines uploads and offloads, ensuring real-time, accurate insights for decision-making. This guide is structured as a "book" with chapters covering everything from basics to advanced management. It's based on official Smartsheet documentation and is current as of August 2025. Data Shuttle requires the Smartsheet Advance Package and specific permissions (e.g., Owner/Admin/Editor on sheets, enabled by System Admins).

If you're new to Smartsheet, review foundational guides first. Let's dive in!

Chapter 1: Overview of Data Shuttle

Data Shuttle automates data transfer, acting as a bridge between Smartsheet and other platforms. It creates workflows to upload data into Smartsheet or offload data out, supporting formats like CSV, XLSX, and Google Sheets. This enables a single source of truth, reducing manual entry and errors.

Key Benefits

- **Automation**: Schedule runs for hands-off operation.
- **Data Transformation**: Filter, map, and merge data during transfer.
- **Integration**: Connects with cloud storage (OneDrive, Google Drive, Box, SharePoint) and systems like ERPs/ CRMs.
- **Security**: Requires permissions; System Admins oversee via

Plan Insights.

- **Efficiency**: Handles large datasets (up to 1GB files, but optimize for 20,000+ rows with DataTables).

Licensing and Requirements

- **Plans**: Included in Smartsheet Advance; contact sales for details.
- **Permissions**: Editor+ on sheets; System Admin enables in Admin Center.
- **Regions/Gov**: Availability varies; Gov users contact support for drives.
- **Limitations**: No support for reports, dashboards, attachments, in-cell images, or circular workflows (to avoid loops).

How It Works

Workflows are upload (import to Smartsheet) or offload (export from Smartsheet). Steps include source/target selection, filtering/mapping, scheduling, and sharing. Runs use UTC time; monitor via dashboards and logs.

Supported Sources and Targets

- **Uploads**: Sources - Smartsheet attachments, OneDrive/SharePoint, Google Drive, Box (CSV/XLSX/Google Sheets). Targets - Smartsheet sheets or DataTables.
- **Offloads**: Sources - Smartsheet sheets. Targets - Smartsheet attachments or external drives (CSV/XLSX).

Advanced Features

- **Triggers**: Manual or scheduled (every 15 mins+).

- **Integrations**: With Control Center for provisioning; Plan Insights dashboard for admins (metrics like workflows, rows updated, errors).
- **Data Handling**: Case-sensitive filters; expressions for transformations.

Example: Upload CRM data to a sales sheet, then offload filtered reports to Google Drive for sharing.

Chapter 2: Ways to Use Data Shuttle

Data Shuttle supports two workflow types: uploads (bring data in) and offloads (send data out). Use cases span industries, focusing on integration, reporting, and archiving.

Upload Workflows

Bring external data into Smartsheet for centralization.

- **Supported Systems/Files**: ERPs, CRMs (non-Salesforce), time-tracking/accounting tools, custom forms; CSV/XLSX/Google Sheets.
- **Examples**:
    - Import hours from time-tracking CSV to project sheets.
    - Merge expenses from XLSX into budgets.
    - Update sales pipelines from CRM Google Sheets.
    - Provision Control Center via intake merges.
    - Import survey data from custom tools.
- **Mapping/Transformations**: Map fields; merge based on keys; filter for relevance (e.g., import only "In Progress" rows).

Offload Workflows

Export Smartsheet data for sharing or ingestion elsewhere.

- **Supported Systems/Files**: Databases, cloud storage

(OneDrive/SharePoint, Google Drive, Box); CSV/XLSX.

- **Examples**:
    - Share status reports with non-users via CSV attachments.
    - Export simplified data for database imports.
    - Weekly reports to cloud for emailing.
    - Filtered data to another sheet for analysis.
    - Archive/audit backups.
- **Mapping/Transformations**: Select columns; filter (e.g., modified rows); format for targets.

Real-World Scenarios

- Project Management: Upload time logs, offload status to stakeholders.
- Finance: Merge expenses, export audits to Box.
- Sales: Update pipelines from CRM, offload leads to databases.

Best Practice: Start with simple merges; use filters to avoid overload.

Chapter 3: Creating Upload Workflows

Upload workflows import data to Smartsheet. Follow these steps:

1. **Access Data Shuttle**: Log in to Smartsheet, then go to the Launcher (top-right apps icon) > Data Shuttle.
2. **Create New Workflow**: Click "Create Workflow" > Select "Upload data to Smartsheet."
3. **Select Source**: Choose the data source – Smartsheet attachment, OneDrive/SharePoint, Google Drive, Box, or Dropbox. Upload a sample file if needed for mapping.
4. **Configure Source**: Authenticate the external service if required; select the file or folder. For recurring, set file

pattern matching (e.g., *report.csv).

5. **Select Target**: Choose the Smartsheet sheet or DataTable to upload to. Create a new sheet if none exists.
6. **Map Fields**: Match source columns to target columns; set transformations (e.g., concatenate, split, or use expressions like UPPERCASE).
7. **Set Upload Options**:
    - Replace all data, append new rows, or merge based on unique identifier (key column).
    - Handle duplicates: Update matching rows, skip, or add as new.
8. **Add Filters**: Optional – Filter rows to import (e.g., only if "Status = Active").
9. **Schedule Runs**: Manual, on file change, or timed (every 15 mins to daily). Set notifications for success/failure.
10. **Test and Save**: Run a test upload; review logs for errors; save and activate.

Advanced Configuration

- **Expressions**: Use formulas in mapping (e.g., CONCAT(source_col1, " - ", source_col2)).
- **Unique ID**: For merges, select a key like "ID" to match rows.
- **Error Handling**: Set fallback values for missing data.

Examples and Tips

- **Scenario**: Import daily sales from CSV – Source: Google Drive folder; Merge on "Date"; Filter > previous day.
- **Tips**: Use sample files for setup; monitor via Plan Insights dashboard.
- **Pitfalls**: Mismatched types cause errors – align formats; large

files (>1GB) fail – split them.

Pro Tip: Combine with automations for post-upload processing.

Chapter 4: Creating Offload Workflows

Offload workflows export data from Smartsheet to external formats or systems.

Step-by-Step Setup

1. **Create Workflow**: In Data Shuttle, "Create Workflow" > "Offload data from Smartsheet."
2. **Select Source**: Choose the Smartsheet sheet; select columns to export.
3. **Configure Filters**: Filter rows (e.g., modified since last run, or "Status = Complete").
4. **Set Target**: Attachment in Smartsheet, or external (OneDrive, Google Drive, etc.); set file name/format (CSV/XLSX).
5. **Map and Transform**: Reorder columns; apply expressions (e.g., format dates).
6. **Schedule**: Manual, on sheet change, or timed.
7. **Test and Activate**: Run test; check output file.

Advanced Features

- **Delta Exports**: Offload only changed rows using "Modified Since Last Run."
- **File Naming**: Dynamic with placeholders (e.g., Report_{{TODAY}}).

Examples and Use Cases

- **Scenario**: Export completed tasks to archive CSV – Filter "Status = Done"; Schedule daily.

- **Advanced**: Offload to ERP – Map to specific formats; integrate with Zapier for further processing.

Tips, Troubleshooting, Pitfalls

- **Tips**: Use for backups; combine with upload for bi-directional sync.
- **Troubleshooting**: No export? Check permissions; errors in logs.
- **Pitfalls**: Sensitive data exposure – restrict access; circular workflows loop – avoid self-referencing.
- **Limitations**: No attachments export; max file size considerations.

Pro Tip: Use offloads for reporting to non-Smartsheet users.

Chapter 5: Managing Data Shuttle Workflows

Manage workflows for efficiency and troubleshooting.

Editing and Running

- Edit: In Data Shuttle dashboard, select workflow > Edit.
- Manual Run: Click "Run Now"; view history/logs.

Transfer Ownership

- Admin: In dashboard, transfer to another user.

Best Practices

- Monitor: Use Plan Insights for usage metrics (rows processed, errors).
- Optimize: Schedule during off-hours; test changes.
- Security: Review permissions; use for compliant data flows.

Troubleshooting

- Errors: Check logs for details (e.g., authentication failed – re-authenticate).
- Slow Runs: Large data – filter more; contact support if persistent.

Limitations and FAQs

- Quotas: Based on Advance plan; contact sales for details.
- FAQs: No real-time sync (min 15 mins); supports up to 1M cells in DataTables.

Pro Tip: Integrate with Control Center for automated provisioning.

This completes the Data Shuttle guide, equipping you to automate data flows seamlessly!

DataMesh Overview

Welcome to this comprehensive guide on DataMesh, a premium add-on for Smartsheet that automates data synchronization across multiple sheets and reports. By mapping lookup values, DataMesh eliminates manual copying, reduces errors like typos, and ensures consistency in one-to-many data relationships without relying on complex formulas. This guide mirrors the structure of the Data Shuttle guide, covering everything from basics to advanced management. It's based on official Smartsheet documentation and is current as of July 25, 2025. DataMesh requires the Smartsheet Advance Package and specific permissions (Viewer+ on source sheets, Admin+ on source reports and target sheets). Access it via the Launcher in Smartsheet or at datamesh.smartsheet.com

If you're new to Smartsheet, review foundational guides first. Let's dive in!

Chapter 1: Overview of DataMesh

DataMesh is a premium application that maps and syncs data between Smartsheet sheets and reports, automating the process of copying or linking values based on unique lookup keys. It creates consistency across datasets, such as pulling employee details from a master HR sheet into project trackers, without duplicative entry or formula maintenance.

Key Benefits

- **Automation and Efficiency**: Syncs data on demand or schedule, reducing manual work and errors.
- **Data Integrity**: Handles one-to-many mappings, duplicates, and updates while preserving formats like hyperlinks and images.
- **Flexibility**: Supports copying data, creating cell links, or

adding new rows—ideal for large-scale data management.
- **Security**: Leverages Smartsheet permissions; System Admins control access via Admin Center.
- **Performance**: Doesn't count toward cell link limits for copy operations (unlike formulas or cell linking mode)

Licensing and Requirements

- **Plans**: Part of Smartsheet Advance Package; additional cost—contact sales for pricing. Available in Commercial and EU regions; not in Gov or AU.
- **Permissions**: Viewer+ on source sheets, Admin+ on source reports and all target sheets. Enable in Admin Center > User Management.
- **Limitations**: Sheets up to 20,000 rows/400 columns; 190 mapped columns max. For larger datasets (>20,000 rows), use DataTable (up to 2M rows). No support for sheet summary reports as sources; all Smartsheet cell limits apply (500,000 cells/sheet, 4,000 chars/cell).

How It Works

Configs define source (sheet/report with master data), target (sheet to update), lookup values (unique keys like IDs), and mapped fields. Runs copy/link/add data based on matches. Triggers: Manual or scheduled (not immediate for reports).

Differences from Formulas

Unlike VLOOKUP/INDEX/MATCH (which create links and hit cell limits), DataMesh's copy modes avoid limits and allow adding new data without formulas.

Chapter 2: Ways to Use DataMesh

DataMesh excels in scenarios requiring consistent data across sheets, such as reference lookups or master-detail syncing. It's best for advanced users managing interconnected workflows.

Upload/Sync Use Cases (Copy/Link Data)

- **Project Planning**: Pull cost/pricing info from a master inventory sheet into project plans using part numbers as lookups.
- **HR Management**: Sync employee details (e.g., phone numbers, addresses) from a central HR sheet to department trackers.
- **Property Management**: Ensure address consistency across lease and maintenance sheets.
- **Sales/CRM**: Update client info from a master list to opportunity sheets.
- **Education**: Sync student IDs and details across enrollment and grade sheets.

Add New Data Use Cases (Copy and Add)

- **Expanding Datasets**: Add new entries from a source report (e.g., new hires) to a target sheet automatically.
- **Merging Sources**: Combine data from multiple sources into a consolidated sheet.

Real-World Scenarios

- **One-to-Many Sync**: A master vendor list (source) updates contact info in multiple project sheets (targets) via vendor ID.
- **Duplicate Handling**: In a source with duplicates, choose to pick the first match or ignore them.

- **Cell Links for Live Updates**: Use for scenarios needing real-time linking, but monitor cell limits.

Best Practice: Use for static lookups; for massive data, pair with DataTable.

Chapter 3: Creating Configurations

Configurations (configs) define the mapping rules. Follow these steps to create one.

Step-by-Step Setup

1. **Access DataMesh**: Open the Launcher in Smartsheet > Select DataMesh. First-time users: Log in at datamesh.smartsheet.com.
2. **Create New**: Click "New Config" in the upper-right.
3. **Select Source**: Search/browse for the sheet/report with master data. Requires Viewer+ (sheet) or Admin+ (report). Note: No sheet summary reports.
4. **Select Target**: Search/browse for the sheet to update. Requires Admin+.
5. **Map Columns**:
    - Choose Lookup Values: Select a common column with unique values in source (e.g., Employee ID). Not copied.
    - Map Fields: Select source and target columns to sync (names don't need to match). Up to 190 columns.
6. **Set Options**:
    - **Overwrite Existing Data**: Yes (updates mismatches) or No (skips existing).
    - **Duplicates in Source**: Pick 1st Match or Ignore Entries.
    - **Data Mapping Format**: Copy Data (simple copy), Create Cell Links (live links, counts toward limits),

Copy and Add Data (copies and adds new rows for unmatched lookups).
    - **Execution Frequency**: Schedule (e.g., hourly, daily); no immediate for reports.
7. **Name and Confirm**: Enter a config name > Review mappings > Update.

Advanced Options and Tips

- **Rich Media**: Copy mode preserves images/hyperlinks; cell links show filenames.
- **Examples**: Map "Phone" from HR source to project target using "Email" as lookup.
- **Pitfalls**: Ensure lookups are unique in source; mismatched types (e.g., date vs. text) block mapping.

Chapter 4: Running Configurations

Once created, run configs manually or on schedule to apply changes.

Step-by-Step Running

1. **Select Config**: From the main DataMesh page, click the config name.
2. **Review Options**: Confirm settings (e.g., overwrite, duplicates).
3. **Run Manually**: Click "Run" > Preview changes (e.g., rows affected, duplicates).
4. **Submit and View Results**: Submit > See summary (total affected/unaffected, new rows) > Close. Refresh target sheet to view.
5. **Scheduled Runs**: If frequency set (e.g., hourly), it auto-runs at next interval.

Viewing Results

- Preview: Details like Total Rows Affected, Duplicates, Not Matched.
- Post-Run Summary: Per-target stats; refresh sheet for updates.

Tips

- For reports as sources, expect delays (no immediate runs).
- Test on small data first; monitor for errors in results.

Chapter 5: Managing and Transferring Configurations

Manage configs via the DataMesh dashboard; transfer ownership when needed.

Management

- **Edit**: Click config > Update options/mappings > Save.
- **Delete**: Remove unused configs (irreversible).
- **Bulk Actions**: For org-wide, submit support ticket.
- **Ownership**: Configs tied to creator; if access revoked, they fail.

Transferring

1. **Requirements**: New owner must have logged into DataMesh, be on same plan, and have Admin+ on source/target.
2. **Steps**: In config > Click Transfer icon > Enter new owner's email > They receive notification > Accept in DataMesh.
3. **Bulk Transfer**: Log support ticket with user details.

Tips

- Transfer before user leaves; ensure permissions.

Chapter 6: Troubleshooting DataMesh

Common issues and fixes:

Behavior	Cause	Resolution
Blank rows added	Rows had data deleted but retain history	Delete entire row via menu.
Periodic failures on immediate update	Server queue or report delays	Wait for next hourly; no action needed.
Fields not copying	Invalid data types, restrictions, system/ predecessor columns	Correct data, remove restrictions, avoid system columns.
No updates in target	Sheet changes (e.g., renamed columns)	Remap in config.
Report as source error	Sheet summary report selected	Use row reports only; contact support if persists.
Config stops working	Owner access revoked/ downgraded	Restore permissions or transfer.

- **General**: If columns renamed, remap. For bulk issues, contact support.

Chapter 7: Best Practices, Limitations, and FAQs

Best Practices

- **Setup**: Use unique lookups; standardize column names; test mappings.
- **Maintenance**: Update configs after sheet changes; transfer ownership proactively; delete unused.
- **Optimization**: For >20,000 rows, use DataTable; avoid reports for immediate needs.
- **Examples**: Sync master lists to trackers; add new data from reports.

Limitations

- No source/target changes post-creation (recreate config).
- Cell links count toward limits; max 190 mapped columns.
- No AU/Gov support; reports can't update immediately.

FAQs (Selected)

- **Permissions?** Viewer+ source sheet, Admin+ report/target.
- **Who can use?** Any user on Advance plan; admins restrict.
- **Formulas vs. DataMesh?** DataMesh avoids limits for copies.
- **Change source/target?** No, recreate.
- **Bulk transfer?** Via support ticket.

This guide equips you to master DataMesh! For hands-on, explore Smartsheet University courses. If needed, pair with tools like Data Shuttle or Control Center.

Pivot App Overview

The Smartsheet Pivot App is a premium add-on tool designed to help users summarize and analyze large datasets from sheets or reports, creating pivot tables to uncover comparisons, patterns, trends, and insights for better decision-making. It functions like a pivot table feature, allowing data aggregation (e.g., sums, averages, counts) without manual updates, and integrates with dashboards for visualization. As of 2025, it's particularly useful for metrics tracking, data categorization, and sharing summarized views with stakeholders, though users have reported occasional issues with automatic updates.

What is the Pivot App?

Pivot App enables the creation of dynamic pivot tables within Smartsheet, transforming raw data into actionable summaries. It's ideal for scenarios like financial reporting, project tracking, or sales analysis, where users need to group data by categories (e.g., by month, department, or status) and apply calculations. Unlike basic sheets, it automates data aggregation and supports features like filters, groupings, and chart integration for dashboards.youtube.com The app outputs results to a new sheet, which can be refreshed manually or on a schedule (e.g., hourly), though "immediate" updates may take 5 minutes to an hour.

Key Features

The app offers robust capabilities for data manipulation and visualization:

- Data Summarization: Calculate sums, averages, counts, mins, maxes, or lists of unique values across columns.
- Grouping and Filtering: Group data by rows/columns (e.g., by date or category) and apply filters to include/exclude specific rows.
- Scheduled Refreshes: Set pivots to update automatically (e.g.,

hourly, daily) or manually, with logs for troubleshooting.

- Output Control: Generates a new sheet for results, allowing sharing without exposing source data; supports charts in dashboards.
- Limitations: Handles up to 500,000 cells in source data; no direct editing of pivot logic in the output sheet.

Eligibility Criteria

Pivot App is available as a premium add-on for users on Business, Enterprise, or Premier plans (or equivalent). It requires a licensed Smartsheet account with editor or higher permissions on the source sheets/reports. System Admins can manage access organization-wide. It's not included in free plans and must be purchased separately.

Benefits for Users

This app enhances productivity and data-driven workflows in several ways:

- Efficient Analysis: Quickly aggregate large datasets without complex formulas, saving time on manual calculations.
- Improved Insights: Identify trends and patterns easily, supporting better decisions in areas like budgeting or performance tracking.
- Seamless Integration: Works with existing Smartsheet tools like reports, dashboards, and automations for end-to-end workflows.
- Controlled Sharing: Share summarized data securely, limiting access to sensitive source information.
- Automation Reliability: Reduces maintenance needs, though community feedback highlights the value of monitoring refresh schedules for real-time accuracy.

How to Join and What to Expect

To get started, contact Smartsheet Sales via https://www.smartsheet.com/contact-us-sales or through your account dashboard to purchase and enable the add-on.

Once activated:

1. Open the Pivot App from the Smartsheet launcher.
2. Select a source sheet or report.
3. Choose rows/columns for grouping, values for calculations, and apply filters.
4. Set refresh frequency and run the pivot to generate the output sheet.
5. Edit or refresh as needed via the app's config logs.

Expect stable performance for most use cases, but for issues like delayed updates, consult Smartsheet Support or the community forums. As of July 2025, recent discussions include calls for enhanced pivot features like native table integration, and updates to refresh reliability.

This app is perfect for data analysts and teams needing advanced summarization in Smartsheet. For the most current details, check the official Smartsheet website or help center.

Resource Management Overview

Welcome to this comprehensive guide on Resource Management by Smartsheet, a premium add-on designed to optimize team capacity, project allocation, and workload balancing. This tool integrates seamlessly with Smartsheet to provide real-time insights into resource availability, helping organizations build effective teams, prevent burnout, and forecast future needs. Formerly known as 10,000ft Plans, it's ideal for project managers, operations leads, and HR professionals managing complex portfolios. This guide is structured as a "book" with chapters, drawing from official Smartsheet resources and documentation as of July 25, 2025. It requires a Business or Enterprise Smartsheet plan with the Resource Management upgrade; contact sales for pricing and licensing. Access it via rm.smartsheet.com or within Smartsheet.

If you're new to Smartsheet, review foundational guides first. Let's dive in!

Chapter 1: Overview of Resource Management

Resource Management by Smartsheet is a resource and project portfolio planning solution that provides visibility into team capacity across an organization's entire work portfolio. It enables users to act on critical data, such as availability and workloads, to ensure projects are staffed appropriately and business goals are met.

Key Features

- **People View**: A centralized dashboard showing who is available and what team members are working on.
- **Capacity View**: Visual heatmaps and tools to balance workloads, identify over/underutilization, and prevent burnout.
- **Time Tracking**: Easy logging of hours for accurate project

estimates and billing.

- **Forecasting**: Proactive staffing needs analysis, skill gap identification, and strategic hiring support.
- **Skill-Based Assignments**: Automatic recommendations for reassignments based on skills, interests, and availability.
- **Pre-Built Reports**: Includes Time + Fees, Expenses, Budgets, and Utilization reports for quick insights.
- **Placeholders**: Flexible planning with role-based allocations that can be replaced later with specific people.
- **Integrations**: Native with Smartsheet for workload tracking; additional tools like calendars and ERPs via API.

Benefits

- **Productivity Boost**: Centralized views accelerate decision-making and resource allocation.
- **Burnout Prevention**: Workload balancing ensures sustainable pacing.
- **Optimized Projects**: Aligns skills with demands for better outcomes.
- **Data-Driven Forecasting**: Improves estimates and hiring with historical time data.
- **Efficiency Gains**: Users report 25% higher utilization and reduced staffing timelines by weeks.

How It Works

The tool organizes resources (people, tools, materials) efficiently by identifying needs, scheduling to avoid conflicts, and adjusting dynamically. It uses visual interfaces like heatmaps for immediate insights and automates recommendations for assignments. Data flows from Smartsheet sheets into Resource Management for analysis, with real-time updates supporting agile adjustments.

Licensing and Requirements

- **Plans**: Add-on for Business/Enterprise; pricing based on users (contact sales).
- **Permissions**: Viewer+ for basic access; Resourcing Administrator for advanced management.
- **Limitations**: Max 20,000 rows/400 columns per integrated sheet; API for custom extensions.10kft.github.io

Chapter 2: Ways to Use Resource Management

Resource Management supports various scenarios in project, HR, and operations workflows, emphasizing human and asset optimization.

Common Use Cases

- **Project Planning**: Assign resources based on skills and availability; use placeholders for early-stage forecasting.
- **HR and Team Building**: Track employee workloads, identify skill gaps, and support hiring.
- **Capacity and Workload Balancing**: Visualize team utilization to resolve overallocations.
- **Time and Expense Tracking**: Log hours/expenses for accurate billing and estimates.
- **Portfolio Oversight**: Monitor multiple projects' resource demands in one view.
- **Forecasting and Reporting**: Analyze data for strategic decisions, like utilization rates or budget adherence.

Industry Examples

- **Manufacturing/Construction**: Manage equipment and labor inventories.
- **Consulting/Services**: Allocate consultants by expertise to

client projects.
- **Education**: Schedule staff for courses and events.
- **IT/Software**: Balance developer workloads across sprints.

Best Practice: Start with human resources (people management) as the core, then expand to assets.

Chapter 3: Getting Started and Setup

Begin with account configuration and data import to unlock core features.

Step-by-Step Setup

1. **Access the Tool**: Log in at rm.smartsheet.com/si using your Smartsheet credentials.
2. **Import Work from Smartsheet**: In the top-right, click "+ Import work from Smartsheet" and follow prompts to connect sheets (e.g., project trackers).
3. **Configure Basic Settings**: As an admin, set company details, time zones, and default schedules.
4. **Add Users/People**: Invite team members via email; assign roles (e.g., Viewer, Editor, Admin).
5. **Set Up Schedules**: Define work hours, holidays, and bill rates.
6. **Request Demo if Needed**: Schedule at smartsheet.com/contact/resource-management-live-demo.

Navigation Basics

- **Dashboards**: People View for individual status; Capacity View for heatmaps.
- **Menus**: Access projects, reports, and settings from the sidebar.
- **Search**: Quickly find people or projects.

Beginner Tips

- Import a small sheet first to test.
- Explore free tutorials in Smartsheet Learning Center.
- Subscribe to release news for updates.

Chapter 4: Managing People and Users

Focus on adding, configuring, and optimizing team members.

Key Features

- **Add/Remove People**: Invite via email; set profiles with skills, rates, and availability.
- **Schedules and Bill Rates**: Customize work calendars and hourly rates.
- **Permissions**: Assign levels like Resourcing Administrator for full control.
- **Skill Profiles**: Tag skills for matching assignments.

Step-by-Step Management

1. **Add User**: Admin > People Settings > Invite; enter email and role.
2. **Edit Profile**: Select user > Update skills, schedule, bill rate.
3. **Manage Permissions**: Set access (e.g., view-only for stakeholders).
4. **Reset Passwords**: Admin tool for security.

Best Practices

- Regularly update skills for accurate recommendations.
- Use groups for bulk permissions.

Chapter 5: Managing Projects

Create and optimize projects with resource allocation.

Key Features

- **Project Creation**: Define timelines, budgets, and phases.
- **Resource Allocation**: Assign people or placeholders; use heatmaps to balance.
- **Tracking**: Monitor progress, costs, and dependencies.
- **Adjustments**: Reassign based on skills or availability.

Step-by-Step

1. **Create Project**: + New Project > Set name, dates, budget.
2. **Allocate Resources**: Drag from People View or use auto-recommend.
3. **Set Dependencies**: Link tasks; enable critical path.
4. **Monitor**: Use Capacity View for issues.

Examples

- Multi-project portfolio: Balance devs across sprints.
- Best Practices: Prioritize high-urgency tasks; level resources to avoid peaks.

Chapter 6: Time Tracking and Reporting

Track effort and analyze data for insights.

Time Tracking

- **Setup**: Enable in settings; define categories.
- **Usage**: Log hours via mobile/web; submit for approval.
- **Approvals**: Managers review/approve timesheets.
- **Reporting**: Generate utilization reports.

Reporting

- **Types**: Time + Fees, Expenses, Budgets, Utilization.
- **Creation**: Select template > Customize filters.
- **Insights**: Export to PDF/Excel; share dashboards.

Best Practices

- Log daily to avoid errors; use for forecasting.

Chapter 7: Integrations and Advanced Configurations

Extend functionality with connections.

Key Integrations

- **Smartsheet**: Import sheets for workload data.
- **Others**: API for ERPs/CRMs; calendars for scheduling.
- **Setup**: Admin > Integrations > Authorize and map fields.10kft.github.io

Advanced

- **Security**: SSO, data encryption.
- **Custom**: Use API for scripts.

Chapter 8: Troubleshooting, Best Practices, and Limitations

Troubleshooting

- **No Data**: Check imports/permissions.
- **Overallocations**: Use heatmaps to resolve.
- **Errors**: View logs; contact support.

Best Practices

- Plan for unknowns; use RACI matrices.
- Monitor KPIs like utilization rate.

- Templates: Use Smartsheet's for budgets/inventories.

Limitations

- Plan-dependent features; no Gov/AU support in some regions.

This guide equips you to master Resource Management! For hands-on, visit Smartsheet Learning Center or request a demo. If needed, explore related tools like Control Center.

Bridge Overview

Smartsheet Bridge is a premium automation and integration tool that enables users to build advanced, triggered workflows for automating repeatable, condition-based processes across Smartsheet, Resource Management, and external systems. It extends beyond standard Smartsheet automations by supporting complex actions like API integrations, JavaScript customization, and cross-system data connections, helping teams eliminate manual tasks and improve efficiency. As of 2025, Bridge continues to focus on scalable, no-code/low-code solutions for enterprise-level workflow management, though no major new features are highlighted in recent documentation.

What is Bridge?

Bridge is a capability within the Smartsheet platform designed to connect data across systems, automate routine tasks, and enhance workflows with greater accuracy and innovation. It's particularly useful for creating complex automations that involve multiple sheets, external APIs, or custom logic, such as sharing sheets or managing user access programmatically. Workflows in Bridge are the core feature, allowing users to gather data from various platforms, apply conditional logic, and trigger actions automatically.

Key Features

Bridge offers a range of tools for building and managing automations:

- **Drag-and-Drop Interface**: Easily assemble workflow blocks without coding expertise.
- **Triggers and Scheduling**: Workflows can start based on events (e.g., sheet changes) or set schedules.
- **Branching Logic**: Customize paths in workflows to handle different conditions and outcomes.

- **API and HTTP Calls**: Integrate with external systems using pre-built modules for APIs, HTTP requests, and JavaScript for added functionality.
- **Integrations**: Supports connections with tools like Google Translate, Resource Management, SharePoint, ServiceNow, and Smartsheet itself.
- **Workflow Management**: Create, view, edit, and delete workflows, workspaces, and authentications.

Eligibility Criteria

Bridge is a paid premium add-on, available for purchase with an Enterprise Smartsheet plan or as part of Smartsheet Advance. It requires an active Smartsheet account, and access is managed by a Bridge System Administrator (typically the primary Smartsheet System Admin). Users must be added individually by the admin, and it's compatible with browsers on PC, Mac, Linux, and mobile devices. There are no additional prerequisites beyond the plan purchase, but it's not included in lower-tier plans like Business or free versions.

Benefits for Users

Bridge provides significant advantages for organizations handling complex processes:

- **Automation at Scale**: Reduces manual work by automating repetitive tasks and integrating disparate systems, freeing teams for higher-value activities.
- **Increased Efficiency and Accuracy**: Connects data flows to minimize errors and provide actionable insights across platforms.
- **Customization Flexibility**: Low-code options allow tailored workflows without needing IT support, supporting innovation and adaptability.
- **Seamless Integration**: Enhances Smartsheet's core features

with external tools, improving overall workflow management.

How to Join and What to Expect

To access Bridge, contact Smartsheet Sales to purchase it for your account. Once purchased, the System Administrator receives a welcome email with a unique URL to the Bridge environment. Admins can then add users and share the URL for access. Getting started involves exploring the Help Center Learning Track for tutorials, templates, and workflow examples. Expect an intuitive interface for building workflows, with support for troubleshooting via Smartsheet's help resources. For any issues or advanced setup, refer to FAQs in the Learning Center.

This tool is ideal for enterprises seeking advanced automation and integration capabilities in Smartsheet. For the most current details, check the official Smartsheet website or help center.

Smartsheet Programs to consider

Smartsheet's Early Adopter Program

Smartsheet, a leading work management platform, offers the Early Adopter Program (EAP) as a way for dedicated users to get a sneak peek at upcoming features and contribute to their development This program is designed for Smartsheet "champions" who are enthusiastic about new releases and enjoy building innovative solutions within the platform. It's an exclusive opportunity for select customers to test and provide feedback on new capabilities before they're rolled out to the general public, helping shape the future of Smartsheet.

What is the Early Adopter Program?

The EAP provides early access to production-grade features and add-ons that have undergone quality assurance but may not yet have full help content or in-product tips available. Participants can explore innovations like AI-powered tools for gaining insights from data in reports, dashboards, or summary sheets useful for quick answers during meetings or presentations. Other recent examples include new dashboard color themes that enhance visual appeal and professionalism. The program operates under a Non-Disclosure Agreement (NDA) to maintain confidentiality, and features are designed not to disrupt existing workflows. There are two enrollment options: individual membership or all-organization access, allowing entire teams to participate if approved.

Eligibility Criteria

To join, you must be a licensed user on a Smartsheet Business, Enterprise, or Premier Plan. Applications require a primary business email associated with your Smartsheet license—ISP domains like @gmail.com or @outlook.com are not eligible. The program is currently available only to users on the default Commercial US plan and is not open to Smartsheet EU or Smartsheet Gov users. System

Administrators can apply to enroll all licensed users in their organization. Spaces are limited, so not every applicant may be accepted.

Benefits for Participants

Being part of the EAP comes with several advantages tailored to power users and organizations looking to stay ahead:

- **Early Access**: Test new features before they're publicly released, giving you a competitive edge in optimizing workflows.
- **Influence Product Development**: Provide direct feedback to Smartsheet's team, helping refine features based on real-world use.
- **Exclusive Resources**: Gain access to webinars, learning materials, and dedicated support for early features.
- **Risk-Free Testing**: Features are stable, and any data added remains intact (though it may become read-only if a feature requires a higher plan post-release).
- **Community Engagement**: Join discussions in the Smartsheet Community group for EAP participants to share experiences and adapt to new tools.

Participants are encouraged to try all features, but you can opt out of specific ones by emailing eap@smartsheet.com.

How to Join and What to Expect

To apply as an individual, visit https://www.smartsheet.com/eap/apply. For organization-wide enrollment, System Admins can use https://www.smartsheet.com/eap/applyorg or contact eap@smartsheet.com. Once accepted, you'll receive email notifications when new features are enabled, along with resources and webinar invites. Feedback is requested to improve the features, and for support, you can reach out to eap@smartsheet.com or check https://help.smartsheet.com/contact.

If you decide to leave the program, simply email eap@smartsheet.com to withdraw at any time. As of recent updates (including a June 2025 overview video), the program continues to evolve, focusing on innovations like AI enhancements.

This program is ideal for Smartsheet enthusiasts eager to drive efficiency and innovation in their teams. If you're eligible, applying could give you a head start on the platform's next big evolutions. For the most current details, check the official Smartsheet website.

Smartsheet's Mobilizer Program

Smartsheet's Mobilizer Program is a free initiative aimed at empowering passionate users to become champions of the platform within their organizations. It provides participants with exclusive tools and support to effectively communicate Smartsheet's value, drive adoption, and foster transformation among peers, business leaders, and IT teams. With over 4,000 members worldwide, the program positions Mobilizers as "change catalysts" who embody Smartsheet's mission to enable anyone to drive meaningful change. It's particularly geared toward power users who want to scale Smartsheet usage, host events, and build consensus for broader implementation. Recent features, such as an Advance adoption dashboard with capability-specific insights, have been added to help members track and optimize platform usage.

What is the Mobilizer Program?

The program equips Smartsheet enthusiasts with resources to share the platform across their organizations, peers, and leadership. It's not just about personal mastery but about evangelizing Smartsheet to accelerate efficiencies and innovation. Participants can host events, educate others, and leverage Smartsheet for organizational success stories evidenced by stats like 94% of Mobilizers crediting Smartsheet for their achievements and 37% seeing promotions tied to their efforts. The program includes access to a private community group in the Smartsheet Community for collaboration and knowledge sharing. It's available only in English as of the latest updates.

Eligibility Criteria

To join, you must be a licensed Smartsheet user on a Business, Enterprise, or Premier plan (or equivalent higher tier). The program is application-based, targeting ambitious, creative customers who are eager to drive transformation. It's open to individuals who can build consensus and promote Smartsheet internally, but spaces may be limited based on demand.

Benefits for Participants

Membership offers a range of advantages for those looking to amplify their impact with Smartsheet:

- **Exclusive Resources**: Pre-built, customizable presentation decks for planning and executing Smartsheet events, along with marketing assets and brand guidelines.
- **Financial Incentives**: Up to $200 annually to motivate peers, such as through giveaways or rewards during events.
- **Community and Networking**: Virtual meet-ups for collaborative growth, private global community groups, and connections with like-minded Mobilizers.
- **Professional Growth**: Opportunities to earn recognition, such as badges in the Smartsheet Community, and contribute to success stories that highlight career advancements.
- **Product Insights**: Access to tools like the Advance adoption dashboard for tracking feature usage and optimizing workflows.
- **Broader Impact**: Helps in gaining executive buy-in, with 100% of surveyed Mobilizers emphasizing its importance for success.

The program also ties into broader initiatives like the Smartsheet Overachievers program, where Mobilizers can earn points and badges for activities like sharing cheat sheets or strategies.

How to Join and What to Expect

Applying is straightforward and free. Visit the official signup page at https://offers.smartsheet.com/mobilizer-program to submit your application. Once accepted, you'll receive access to the Mobilizer Toolkit, community groups, and event resources. Expect virtual meet-ups, ongoing support, and opportunities to share your experiences such as featuring user-created content like cheat sheets in the broader network. There's no strict commitment beyond actively promoting Smartsheet, but participants are encouraged to engage regularly.

If you withdraw, you can simply contact Smartsheet support, though details aren't explicitly outlined. As of February 2025, the program continues to evolve with community-driven content, like shared cheat sheets for beginners.

This program is perfect for Smartsheet advocates wanting to expand its reach and unlock personal and organizational growth. For the latest details, check the official Smartsheet website or community.

Smartsheet Community

The Smartsheet Community is a vibrant online platform that connects users worldwide to drive achievements through Smartsheet. It serves as a hub for peer-to-peer support, where members can ask questions, share best practices, discuss work management trends, receive guidance from experts and fellow users, and provide feedback to shape the future of Smartsheet products. With thousands of active participants, it's a space for collaboration, learning, and innovation, integrating elements like badges, points, and newsletters to enhance engagement. Recent highlights include the ENGAGE conference, where community members can network in person, and updates like new help videos and best practices.

What is the Smartsheet Community?

This free, interactive forum empowers Smartsheet users to unlock the platform's full potential through shared resources and discussions. It's more than a support site it's a community-driven ecosystem focusing on topics like project management, AI-powered features, and workflow optimization. Key integrations include programs like Smartsheet Overachievers, which requires community membership and participation in other initiatives for eligibility, rewarding top contributors with recognition and perks. The community also ties into events like ENGAGE and features updates, such as the ability to mute posts for better notification control, introduced in mid-2025.

Main Features and Sections

The community is organized into various categories and tools to facilitate interaction:

- **Discussions and Topics**: Browse or follow areas like "Ask a Question," "Ideas + Feature Requests" for voting on enhancements, "Show + Tell" for sharing successes, and filtered views for unanswered queries.

- **Resources**: Access customer resources, help articles, and the Help and Learning Center for tutorials and best practices.
- **Profile and Notifications**: Personalize profiles, adjust settings, subscribe to email digests, bookmark posts, and mention users (@username).
- **Formatting and Tools**: Use rich text, hyperlinks, screenshots (without sensitive data), and mark answers as "Insightful" or "Best Answer."
- **Rank and Rewards**: Earn points for activities like posting and answering, unlocking badges (e.g., "Fully Charged" for completing orientation) to celebrate power users.

Eligibility Criteria

The community is open to Smartsheet customers, partners, and users, including those on free or paid plans. No strict eligibility beyond having a Smartsheet account is mentioned, though full participation (e.g., viewing profiles) requires logging in. For tied programs like Overachievers, members must actively participate in the community and other Smartsheet initiatives.

Benefits for Participants

Joining the Smartsheet Community offers numerous advantages for beginners and experts alike:

- **Knowledge Sharing**: Get quick answers, learn best practices, and troubleshoot issues through peer discussions.
- **Product Influence**: Vote on or submit feature ideas to directly impact Smartsheet's development.
- **Recognition and Rewards**: Earn points, badges, and potentially advance to programs like Overachievers for career-boosting visibility (e.g., 94% of Mobilizers credit Smartsheet for achievements, though tied to related programs).

- **Networking**: Connect globally, subscribe to newsletters like Community Corner, and attend events like the annual ENGAGE conference.
- **Enhanced Control**: Features like muting posts and customizable notifications improve user experience.
- **Safe Environment**: Guidelines ensure respectful interactions, with moderation for violations.

Participants are encouraged to search before posting, be descriptive, and disclose AI-generated content for transparency.

How to Join and What to Expect

To join, create or log in with a Smartsheet account at https://community.smartsheet.com/[1] it's free and straightforward. New members should follow the Orientation Checklist: personalize your profile, introduce yourself in "Show + Tell," follow topics, vote on ideas, and engage in discussions. Expect a welcoming environment governed by guidelines that promote respect, prohibit spam/trolling, and require safe sharing (e.g., no personal data or external contacting without permission). Report issues via the "Flag" icon for moderator review.

Once active, you'll receive email notifications, weekly digests, and access to troubleshooting FAQs for common issues like editing posts or updating profiles. The community evolves with updates, such as 2025's new videos and best practices in the Help Center, enhancing learning and participation. For advertising Smartsheet-related services, use the Job Board sparingly (once per quarter).

This community is ideal for anyone seeking to maximize Smartsheet's value through collaboration and growth. For the latest details, visit the official Smartsheet Community website.

---

1. https://community.smartsheet.com/%E2%80%94it's

Advice from the author

Ensuring Governance in Your Smartsheet System

As organizations scale their use of Smartsheet from managing simple tasks to orchestrating enterprise-wide processes, establishing robust governance becomes critical. Governance in a Smartsheet system encompasses the policies, processes, controls, and best practices that ensure the platform is used securely, compliantly, and efficiently across teams. For companies, effective governance safeguards sensitive data, mitigates risks, enforces consistent standards, maximizes return on investment, and fosters innovation while maintaining control. Without it, challenges like uncontrolled data sprawl, unauthorized access, inconsistent workflows, or compliance violations can emerge, leading to operational inefficiencies, security breaches, or even legal repercussions. This section provides an in-depth guide to implementing governance, leveraging Smartsheet's built-in features, and tailoring strategies to meet corporate needs, ensuring your Smartsheet system remains a secure and scalable asset.

Why Governance Matters for Companies

Smartsheet often serves as a central hub for critical business data, including financial forecasts, project portfolios, customer records, and operational metrics. As usage grows, so does the complexity of managing access, ensuring compliance, and maintaining data integrity. Governance addresses these challenges by providing a structured framework to:

- **Protect Data Integrity and Security**: Prevent unauthorized access, data leaks, or accidental modifications that could compromise sensitive information.
- **Ensure Regulatory Compliance**: Align with standards like

GDPR, HIPAA, SOC 2, or industry-specific regulations through auditable processes and controls.

- **Enhance Operational Efficiency**: Standardize workflows, reduce redundant processes, and eliminate manual errors to streamline operations.
- **Enable Scalability**: Support organizational growth by centralizing management, automating oversight, and ensuring the system adapts to evolving needs.
- **Mitigate Risks**: Proactively identify vulnerabilities, such as over-sharing or outdated permissions, and address them before they escalate.
- **Drive Adoption and ROI**: Create trust in the platform by enforcing clear guidelines, encouraging consistent use, and demonstrating value to stakeholders.

For enterprises, a centralized or shared governance model—where IT oversees platform-wide settings and business units manage their specific use cases—offers the best balance of control and flexibility. Smaller companies may start with a simpler, centralized approach, evolving as their Smartsheet footprint expands. Regardless of size, a governance strategy should align with your organization's industry, regulatory requirements, and strategic goals.

Key Components of Smartsheet Governance

Effective governance in Smartsheet hinges on five core pillars: data retention and management, sharing and access controls, security practices, identity and user management, and compliance and auditing. Below, we explore each in detail, including practical steps, tools, and considerations.

1. Data Retention and Management

Unmanaged data accumulation can lead to storage bloat, increased costs, and compliance risks, especially when retaining data beyond legal or business requirements. Smartsheet's Data Retention Controls empower System Administrators to implement organization-wide policies that automatically manage the lifecycle of sheets, reports, dashboards, and other assets.

- **Policy Configuration**: Admins can create retention policies to identify and delete unused or aging assets based on criteria like creation date, last modified date, or access frequency. For example, a policy might flag sheets untouched for 12 months for deletion, notifying owners 30 days in advance.
- **Owner Notifications**: Before deletion, Smartsheet sends automated email alerts to content owners, allowing them to review and retain critical assets if needed. This ensures no essential data is lost accidentally.
- **Exemptions**: Designate specific sheets, workspaces, or folders as exempt from retention policies to protect mission-critical data, such as annual financial reports or compliance documentation.
- **Backup Integration**: Pair retention policies with Smartsheet's backup features to export data to local storage or cloud services (e.g., Google Drive, Box) before deletion, ensuring recoverability.
- **Retention Logs**: Admins can access detailed logs to track which assets were flagged, notified, or deleted, providing transparency and auditability.

Practical Steps:

- Conduct a data audit to understand your organization's Smartsheet asset inventory and identify retention needs.
- Start with conservative policies (e.g., targeting assets unused for 18 months) and refine based on user feedback.
- Schedule policies to run weekly or monthly to keep the

system lean without overwhelming users.

- Train content owners to respond to retention notifications promptly and use exemptions strategically.

Considerations: Balance compliance requirements (e.g., retaining financial data for seven years) with storage optimization. For regulated industries, consult legal teams to align policies with data retention laws.

2. Sharing and Access Controls

Uncontrolled sharing is a leading cause of data exposure in collaborative platforms. Smartsheet provides robust tools to regulate who can access, view, or edit assets, ensuring sensitive information remains secure while enabling collaboration.

- **Safe Sharing**: Restrict sharing to approved domains or email addresses, preventing external leaks. For example, limit sharing to @yourcompany.com or pre-approved partner domains.
- **Data Egress Policies**: Control how data leaves Smartsheet by restricting actions like exporting sheets to Excel, printing reports, or publishing dashboards publicly. This is critical for industries handling personal or proprietary data.
- **Permission Levels**: Use Smartsheet's granular permissions—Viewer (read-only), Editor (modify data), Admin (manage settings), and Owner (full control)—to assign appropriate access. For instance, grant Viewer access to executives for dashboards while reserving Editor rights for project managers.
- **Dynamic View**: Share filtered or specific data with stakeholders without exposing the entire sheet. Ideal for vendors or cross-functional teams needing limited visibility.
- **Attachment and Publish Controls**: Regulate file attachments (e.g., block unapproved file types) and disable

public publishing for sensitive assets to prevent unauthorized distribution.

- **Access Monitoring**: Generate Sheet Access Reports and Published Items Reports to review who has access to what and revoke permissions as needed. For example, identify and remove access for departed employees.

Practical Steps:

- Create an allow list of approved domains and review it quarterly.
- Set default sharing permissions to Viewer for new sheets to minimize over-sharing.
- Use Dynamic View for external collaborators to reduce reliance on full sheet sharing.
- Schedule monthly access reviews to clean up outdated permissions, especially after team changes.

Considerations: Overly restrictive sharing can hinder collaboration, so involve business units in defining policies. For global companies, account for cross-border sharing regulations when configuring domain restrictions.

3. Security Practices

Smartsheet's enterprise-grade security foundation—built on AES 256-bit encryption at rest, TLS encryption in transit, and regular third-party audits—provides a strong starting point for governance. Companies can enhance this with additional controls tailored to their risk profile.

- **Customer Managed Encryption Keys (CMEK)**: For organizations requiring ultimate control, CMEK allows you to manage your own encryption keys, ensuring even

Smartsheet cannot access your data without permission.

- **Automation Permissions**: Restrict who can create workflows that interact with external systems via Bridge or API calls, preventing unauthorized data flows.
- **Web Content Widget Controls**: Limit embedded content in dashboards to trusted sources, reducing risks from malicious scripts or unverified URLs.
- **Vulnerability Management**: Smartsheet conducts regular penetration tests and maintains a vulnerability disclosure program. Companies should complement this by limiting production system access to authorized personnel only.
- **System Status Monitoring**: Subscribe to Smartsheet's status notifications to stay informed about incidents, maintenance, or outages, enabling proactive response planning.

Practical Steps:

- Enable CMEK if your industry (e.g., finance, healthcare) demands strict data sovereignty.
- Restrict automation creation to trained users or admins to prevent unintended integrations.
- Conduct annual security training for users, emphasizing phishing awareness and safe sharing.
- Set up a dedicated IT role to monitor status updates and coordinate incident responses.

Considerations: Security must balance protection with usability. Overly complex controls can frustrate users, so test configurations in a sandbox environment before rolling out organization-wide.

4. Identity and User Management

Centralized identity management prevents shadow IT, ensures only authorized users access Smartsheet, and simplifies onboarding/

offboarding. Smartsheet's identity tools integrate seamlessly with corporate systems, enhancing governance.

- **Single Sign-On (SSO)**: Support for SAML, Google, Microsoft, or Apple SSO streamlines authentication and enforces corporate identity policies. SSO reduces password fatigue and ensures consistent access control.
- **Multi-Factor Authentication (MFA)**: Add an extra layer of security by requiring secondary verification (e.g., via authenticator apps) for all users, especially admins.
- **User Auto Provisioning (UAP)**: Automatically provision or deprovision Smartsheet accounts based on directory changes in tools like Azure AD or Okta, ensuring no orphaned accounts remain after employee departures.
- **Directory Integrations**: Sync with identity providers to manage user attributes, roles, and groups, reducing manual admin work.
- **Role Management**: Assign roles strategically:
    - **System Admins:** Oversee platform settings; maintain at least two for redundancy.
    - **Group Admins**: Manage specific user groups for decentralized control.
    - **Licensed Users**: Grant licenses only to active contributors to optimize costs.
- **API Token Control**: Set expiration dates for API tokens and monitor their usage to prevent unauthorized integrations.

Practical Steps:

- Mandate SSO as the only authentication method to eliminate local password risks.
- Enable MFA for all users, prioritizing admins and users with

access to sensitive data.

- Use UAP to automate user lifecycle management, integrating with your HR system for real-time updates.
- Review API token usage monthly to revoke unused or expired tokens.

Considerations: For large organizations, directory integrations require IT expertise to set up. Test provisioning rules to avoid accidental account deletions. Budget for licensed users carefully, as overuse can inflate costs.

5. Compliance and Auditing

Meeting regulatory and internal compliance requirements demands visibility into Smartsheet usage and robust auditing capabilities. Smartsheet's compliance tools help companies maintain accountability and demonstrate adherence to standards.

- **Event Reporting**: Access a JSON feed tracking over 120 user activities, such as logins, sheet modifications, or sharing actions. Integrate with Security Information and Event Management (SIEM) systems like Splunk for real-time monitoring and alerts.
- **Activity Logs**: Review detailed logs of user actions, including timestamps and IP addresses, to investigate incidents or verify compliance.
- **Access Reviews**: Regularly audit who has access to sheets, workspaces, or reports, ensuring alignment with least-privilege principles.
- **Certifications**: Smartsheet maintains ISO 27001, SOC 2 Type II, and Privacy Shield certifications, supporting compliance with global regulations like GDPR, CCPA, or HIPAA.
- **Data Residency**: Choose data centers in regions that align

with your compliance needs (e.g., US or EU), leveraging Smartsheet's geographically isolated AWS facilities for redundancy and business continuity.

Practical Steps:

- Set up Event Reporting to feed into your SIEM for proactive monitoring.
- Schedule quarterly access reviews, focusing on high-risk assets like financial sheets.
- Document compliance processes in a Smartsheet workspace for auditor access.
- Test disaster recovery plans annually, simulating data restoration from backups.

Considerations: Compliance requirements vary by industry and region, so engage legal and compliance teams early. For regulated sectors, prioritize features like CMEK and Event Reporting to meet audit demands.

Implementing Governance: A Step-by-Step Approach

To establish governance in your Smartsheet system, follow this structured approach, tailored to corporate environments:

1. **Conduct a Baseline Assessment**:
    - Audit current Smartsheet usage: Identify active users, assets, sharing permissions, and integrations.
    - Map regulatory and business requirements to pinpoint governance priorities (e.g., HIPAA for healthcare, GDPR for EU customers).
    - Engage stakeholders (IT, legal, business leaders) to align on goals.
2. **Define Your Governance Model**:
    - Choose between centralized (IT-driven) or shared

(IT oversees, business units manage) governance based on your organization's structure.
- Document policies for data retention, sharing, security, identity, and compliance in a governance charter.
- Assign a governance lead (e.g., a System Admin) to oversee implementation.

1. **Configure Smartsheet Controls**:
    - Set up Data Retention Controls with clear deletion schedules and exemptions.
    - Enable Safe Sharing, Data Egress Policies, and permission defaults to lock down access.
    - Activate SSO, MFA, and UAP for identity management.
    - Configure Event Reporting and integrate with SIEM for compliance monitoring.
2. **Train and Communicate**:
    - Develop training materials using Smartsheet's Learning Center resources, covering policies and best practices.
    - Host workshops for users, admins, and content owners to build governance awareness.
    - Create a governance dashboard in Smartsheet to share updates, track compliance metrics, and gather feedback.
3. **Automate Oversight**:
    - Use Bridge to create workflows that enforce governance rules, such as alerting admins to unauthorized sharing or flagging overdue retention actions.
    - Automate user provisioning/deprovisioning to

reduce manual errors.
    - Schedule recurring reports (e.g., Sheet Access Reports) to streamline audits.
4. **Monitor and Refine**:
    - Use Enterprise Plan Manager to centralize oversight of licenses, permissions, and usage.
    - Review governance metrics monthly, such as policy violations, retention actions, or access anomalies.
    - Solicit user feedback to identify friction points and adjust policies for usability.
    - Conduct annual governance reviews to incorporate new Smartsheet features or regulatory changes.

Advanced Governance Strategies

For mature Smartsheet deployments, consider these advanced tactics to elevate governance:

- **Center of Excellence (CoE)**: Establish a Smartsheet CoE, comprising IT, business, and power users, to drive best practices, oversee governance, and champion adoption. Use the Mobilizer Program to recruit internal advocates.
- **Custom Analytics**: Build dashboards with the Pivot App to visualize governance metrics, such as user activity, sharing trends, or compliance status, for executive reporting.
- **Integration Governance**: For organizations using Bridge or APIs, create a registry of integrations and monitor their data flows to prevent unauthorized connections.
- **Change Management**: Pair governance with a change management plan to support new feature rollouts, using the Early Adopter Program to test updates in a controlled environment.
- **Community Engagement**: Leverage the Smartsheet

Community to share governance templates, learn from peers, and contribute to feature requests that enhance control capabilities.

Challenges and Mitigation Strategies

Implementing governance isn't without hurdles. Common challenges include:

- **User Resistance**: Strict policies may frustrate users accustomed to flexibility. Mitigate by involving users in policy design, offering training, and highlighting governance benefits (e.g., data security).
- **Resource Constraints**: Governance requires time and expertise. Start with high-impact areas (e.g., sharing controls) and scale incrementally, using automation to reduce admin burden.
- **Evolving Needs**: As Smartsheet usage grows, governance must adapt. Establish a feedback loop via surveys or community forums to stay aligned with user and regulatory demands.

Conclusion

By prioritizing governance, your company can transform Smartsheet into a secure, compliant, and efficient platform that drives productivity while minimizing risks. A well-governed Smartsheet system not only protects your data but also empowers teams to innovate with confidence, ensuring long-term value from your investment. Start small with core controls, engage stakeholders, and evolve your strategy as your organization grows. For additional guidance, explore Smartsheet's Help Center, connect with certified partners, or join the Smartsheet Community to learn from global peers.

About the Author

Ken is a passionate advocate for efficient work management and process improvement, bringing 6 years of experience in Smartsheet project coordination and technology integration to this guide. Dedicated to empowering users of all levels, Ken combines practical insights with a deep understanding of Smartsheet's capabilities to help individuals and businesses thrive. His experience and knowledge has benefited companies such as Goltens Worldwide, Elevance Health and currently General Electric Aerospace.

Smartsheet Recognitions:

2022 System Administrator Certification

Smartsheet Automagician2022: a user who has mastered the platform's automation features and is recognized for their ability to create time-saving workflows. Specifically, it's a product usage badge awarded to the top 5% of Smartsheet users who actively utilize automation. These users leverage automation to streamline tasks, reduce manual effort, and improve overall efficiency within their workflows.

Smartsheet Community Ambassador 2022: an active and knowledgeable member of the Smartsheet Community who has earned a high rank (1000 points and 100 posts) and is recognized for their expertise, helpfulness, and engagement. They are a go-to resource for other users, sharing best practices, providing support, and contributing to the overall growth of the community.

Smartsheet Superstar 2023: a user who is recognized for their advanced skills and contributions within the Smartsheet platform. They are not only proficient in using Smartsheet's core features like workflows, forms, reports, and dashboards to create efficient solutions, but they also actively share their knowledge and expertise to help others within their organization utilize the platform effectively.

Special Thanks:

To my wonderful and lovely wife for inspiring me to do what I love and for listening to me constantly talk about Smartsheet.

To my Mentor Robert Harrington for introducing me to Smartsheet and pushing me to learn the platform in 2019.

If you or your organization are looking for lessons or troubleshooting, please reach out to: Smartsheetdude@gmail.com

References

[1] Smartsheet. (2025, July 7). Release Notes - Additional Column Links. Smartsheet.com. Retrieved from web search results.

[2] Smartsheet. (2025, July 10). Smartsheet Forward 2025 Edition 2: Shaping the Future of Enterprise Work. Smartsheet.com. Retrieved from web search results.

[3] Smartsheet. (2025, March 4). Smartsheet Forward 2025 Edition 1: Built for Better Work. Smartsheet.com. Retrieved from web search results.

[4] Smartsheet Developers & API. (2025, June 9). Changelog - Event Types Update. Developers.smartsheet.com. Retrieved from web search results.

[5] Stackby. (2025, May 9). Smartsheet Project Management: Features Guide in 2025. Stackby.com. Retrieved from web search results.

[6] The Digital Project Manager. (2025, June 18). Smartsheet Review 2025: Top Features, Expert Opinion, + Demo. Thedigitalprojectmanager.com. Retrieved from web search results.

[7] Smartsheet. (2025, June 23). Release Notes - Modern Forms Experience. Smartsheet.com. Retrieved from web search results.

[8] Reddit. (2024, September 27). Smartsheet Pricing - 2025. Reddit.com/r/smartsheet. Retrieved from web search results.

Note: All references are based on publicly available information as of August 3, 2025. For the most current details, visit Smartsheet's official release notes.

www.ingramcontent.com/pod-product-compliance
Lightning Source LLC
LaVergne TN
LVHW100317210926
848480LV00003B/1157

* 9 7 9 8 2 3 1 7 7 0 0 1 4 *